Short Stories for the Long Road

Living Scripture in Every Day Life

Susan Sienkiewicz

Find us at:
Sienkreation@gmail.com, Facebook: @sienkreation

Take a minute to pause and walk with God through this garden of unique short stories. Sensitive to the Spirit, Sue shares life events resulting in relatable and powerful moments with God. She has a gift for making the scriptures come alive with everyday living examples of things we all face. Her stories bring clarity to the scriptures allowing you to be encouraged and inspired to wrap God's Word around your own situations and feel His loving warmth fill your soul.

Joann Gammichia
Director of Talent Management,
Former Pastor, Calvary Assembly of God, Winter Park, FL

This book will inspire you, enlighten you, make you laugh and make you cry. The Thought for the Day is more like a prayer utilizing the names of God which draws us to know Him more in our daily lives. Thank you Susan for these amazing stories and life lessons which teach us more about the heart and character of the Lord.

Apostle Jane Hamon
Pastor, Vision Church@Christian International
Santa Rosa Beach, FL

Short Stories for the Long Road is an amazing collection of stories filled with the revelation of God's precious wisdom. They are truly God inspired and will help you to see how scripture verses can bring direction to your life. These stories are revolutionary and uniquely written to inspire. They bring new meaning to our lives, help us to be strengthened, and motivate us to fulfill the dreams God has placed in us.

Pastor Eric Melwani
Senior Pastor, Church Of Many Waters
Orlando, FL

In this book, Susan Sienkiewicz presents powerful stories that are filled with spiritual insight. *Short Stories for the Long Road* is sure to inspire and encourage you. I believe the revelation inside of this book has the potential to greatly impact your life.

Pastor Joshua Gay
Lead Pastor, High Praise Orlando
Orlando, FL

✝ DEDICATION ✝

I am so blessed by God. He has given me faithful friends, and such an amazing family and husband. All that, *and* I have a heavenly Father who has given me a love for writing. It is all about you God, and I dedicate Short Stories for the Long Road to You. You are the real author; all my thanks and praise goes to You!

Contents

Contents

❧ FOREWORD ❧

God created each day to be a gift. Along the path of each day are scattered precious moments, jewels in our crown of life. With only a casual glance, jewels can look like ordinary stones and we can walk right past them never seeing their value. That is unless one takes the time to step beyond the casual gaze and really focus on each stone in turn.

In Short Stories for the Long Road, Susan Sienkiewicz takes the time to not only focus on each stone, but to pick each one up gently and thoughtfully, dust it off, and peer deep inside, finding the hidden beauty in each one. Each devotional is a jewel of great value, found in the seemingly ordinary places of Susan's life. It is her ability to remain keenly aware of the opportunities for learning life's lessons as she navigates the joys and challenges of each day that reveals her hidden treasures.

As you read, take your time and meditate on the similarities and differences in your own life experiences. It is the time you take that will bring value to each moment as you begin filling your own treasure chest with jewels you may have otherwise missed along your path.

Pastor Steve Sienkiewicz
Co-Owner, Sienkreation
Orlando, Florida, August 31, 2017

✝ Preface ✝

I have ended every story with a "Thought for the Day". Each thought begins with one of the names of God. Biblical names carry meanings and describe the nature and attributes of the person who bears that name. I found that learning His names and their meanings was a great way to get to know God on a more personal level. Picture Him as a beautiful diamond with each brilliant facet representing one of His names.

Yahweh - Lord, Jehovah
Elohim – Creator, Mighty and Strong
Immanuel – I Am
El Shaddai - Lord God Almighty
Adonnai - Lord, Master
El Elyon - The Most High God
El Olam – The Everlasting God
Jehovah Nissi- The Lord My Banner
Jehovah Raah - The Lord My Shepherd
Jehovah Rapha - The Lord Who Heals
Jehovah Shammah – The Lord Is There
Jehovah Tsidkenu - The Lord Our Righteousness
Jehovah Mekoddishkem - The Lord Who Sanctifies
Jehovah Jireh – The Lord Will Provide
Jehovah Shalom - The Lord Is Peace
Jehovah Sabaoth - The Lord Of Armies
Jehovah El Roi – The God Who Sees Me
Jehovah Rohi - The Lord Is My Shepherd

🕭 ACKNOWLEDGMENTS 🕭

I am eternally grateful to be able to put my thanks in writing to all who helped to make the dream of this book come to fulfillment. Thank you to my daughter Kimberly Moore and my daughter in law Emily Sienkiewicz who helped in the editing process through their pregnancies and busy schedules. Your encouragement helped more than you know!

Thank you to my spiritual daughter, Christiana La Croix, who would take whatever mess I gave her and make it beautiful. You will always be special to me.

I think everyone should have a friend like the one I have in Johnnie Cunningham. With each new story I wrote, I would call her day or night, read it to her hot off the press. She would *always* stop what she was doing to listen and encourage. Thank you, my forever friend.

Many thanks to my dear friends Debbie and Roger Hawkins. They are my heaven sent cheerleaders, always there with an encouraging word and support.

Words are not enough to thank the love of my life; my husband Steven. Without him, I never could have completed this project. His encouragement and endless hours of working on this is just another way he shows me how much he loves me. He was patient and long suffering, especially when I messed up and sent him the wrong copies. He worked on them for days (and nights) before we realized the error and had to start all over again!

❧ Introduction ☙

This book is a culmination of the heart and mind connection that transpired through the circumstances I encountered on the Road. We each have our own path to travel; we each have our own story. As fellow sojourners, we need to encourage each other, sharing what we have learned in our travels. Short Stories for the Long Road is my encouragement to you. With every circumstance I encountered, I found a scripture that drew me into the understanding of how to get through whatever challenge I was facing.

Imagine starting your day by opening this book and finding an encouraging word to carry you through the day as you sip your morning coffee. I hope that you will be as blessed reading these stories as I was in writing them.

102 YEARS OF GRACE

Isaiah 55:6 (NLT)

Seek the Lord while you can find him.
Call on him now while he is near.

I worked at a retirement home for seven years. One memory I will never forget involved a one hundred and two year old lady. Through conversations in our staff meetings I learned she was cranky, outspoken, and, to say the least, unfriendly. Several people on staff had tried to visit and cheer her up but she told them to leave. Though she didn't want visitors, I felt especially called to go visit this woman. I knew that God had opened the door for me because she let me come in. I was very careful not to stay long, and with each succeeding visit she would let her walls down just a little until one day she actually let me touch her. I would softly stroke her hair and run out before she had time to change her mind about me.

Then the big day came, I was pumped up and ready. I got the nerve to ask her the BIG question about where she believes she will go will go when she dies. As soon as I mentioned God, she said I had crossed the boundary line and it was time for me to go.

I started back at square one with quick visits and eventually built up my courage again. I couldn't help thinking that I didn't have a lot of time since she was one hundred and two. One day I asked her if I could pray for her and to my surprise she said yes. I said a quick prayer and was on my way, only this time I was encouraged. I thought that at last my love was softening her heart.

The next day I went in guns a blazing! I began to talk to her about Jesus. She immediately tried to shut me down but I gathered up the courage to keep going. I asked her why she was so anti–God. She said, "I have been asking Him for years to let me die. I am laying here unable to move and in pain. What kind of God would let me go through all this and not let me die?" God put His words in my mouth; I said, "Only a God of mercy and grace would give you one hundred and two years to find Him. He desires that none should perish but have everlasting life." This time she did throw me out. I left feeling frustrated and wondering what it would take to ever penetrate that wall of hurt, rebellion, and stubbornness.

I waited a few days and then, as I set my path to go to her room, I felt quickened by the Holy Spirit to turn around and go visit others. God sends messengers to speak of His love and His grace, but if we are not received (especially after numerous attempts) He may have us turn around and go in another direction.

It was not long after my last visit that I heard the news that my one hundred and two year old friend had passed away. I can only pray that my words had planted seeds and she received Jesus before she died.

My husband and I used to oversee the homeless ministry at our church. One Sunday morning, I prayed with a young girl. The following week we received news that she had been murdered. I cried as I heard the news, but I also shed tears of joy because I knew she had asked Jesus to come into her heart the week before.

Some people think there is always time and that they will deal with all that "God stuff" later. However, whether we are young, or are given one hundred and two years to make up our minds, we must "Seek Him while He can still be found."

Thought for the Day:

Adonai (My Great Lord) Help me to make You Lord of my life, my first priority, my first love.

Pray for the veil to be lifted and hearts to be softened over those who don't know you.

A FISH STORY

2 Peter 3:18 (ESV)

But grow in the grace and knowledge of our Lord and Savior Jesus Christ. To him be the glory, both now and to the day of eternity. Amen.

While sitting at the lake not far from my house, my eyes were drawn to a fisherman standing nearby. He was so involved in what he was doing; he hadn't noticed that anyone joined his picture of solitude. I thought about how much patience it takes to be a fisherman, sometimes waiting for hours without as much as a tug on the line, yet how rewarding when the "big" one comes!

Suddenly, the water began to move in different directions. I watched with great excitement as the struggle between man and fish began. My imagination grew as I watched the pole bending, almost touching the water. Surely, this would be a fish to tell stories about! The fisherman and I waited expectantly for the truth of the catch to surface. Much to the fisherman's chagrin, the fish was too small and so was thrown back into the water, allowing it to grow for another time and another fish story.

God is like that patient fisherman with us. He reaches his hand toward us and waits patiently for us to take the bait. Sometimes He reels us in and checks our growth. Unlike the disappointed fisherman, He places us carefully back into the stream with great anticipation of our growth as we continue to follow Him. He knows that one day we will be the prize catch, the one worth waiting for.

Thought for the Day:

El Roi (The God Who Sees Me) You know the good, the bad, and everything in between in me. Thank You for being patient with me as I continue to learn from my mistakes. Help me to forgive myself on my journey.

JOURNEY TO WHOLENESS

Psalm 31:7 (NLT)

I am overcome with joy because of your unfailing love, for You have seen my troubles and You care about the anguish of my soul. You have not handed me over to the enemy but have set me in a safe place.

Escaping from the world for a little while, we headed to the beach. For my husband and me it is the best place to get away from it all. When we arrived we noticed that the ocean banks were strewn with shells of every shape and size.

Living in Florida, it is not unusual to see shells, but this day was different. There was a blanket of shells, so many that we found ourselves like children in a candy store. We filled our pockets with our favorite ones. Many were replaced as we found ones that were more colorful or less broken. We set out to find the perfect shell.

I picked up one broken shell after another. I began to picture each shell leaving the shelter of the seabed, and being tossed about in crashing waves and bumping against the jagged rocks. How rare it would be to find one that had survived the elements of the sea and remained in one piece!

It reminded me of a baby fully protected in its mother's womb, having to leave that safe place and start its arduous journey through the birth canal. The baby then makes his arrival into the hands of the doctor who immediately checks for any flaws.

We are in awe as the fingers and toes are counted and breathe a sigh of relief at such perfection.

Like the shell, few of us have remained unbroken and whole since our emergence into the world. We are as fragile as the shells, easily cracked and broken as we bump against the rocks of life. Like the shells, we have different levels of brokenness.

For some of us, it seems the journey through life has been one riptide after another, a force constantly trying to pull us under and drown us. It is though we are caught in a hurricane at sea, thrown and tossed about, only to end up crashing on the coastline shattered and broken.

As I looked more closely at each shell I began to see a beauty I hadn't noticed before. Everywhere the shell had been broken, it's once jagged edges were smooth, shiny and polished from the waters that had flowed over them day after day.

I think God looks down from heaven and sees His creation shattered and weathered from life's storms. Unlike the imperfect shells that are left behind, He bends down and picks us up. We are exactly what He is looking for. We are His favorite. He has a whole collection of broken shells. Unlike the shells that can never be put back together again, He has the power to make us whole. He saves every piece in His hands. He will pour the living waters of His Spirit over us and in time we will become smooth and shiny, and reflect the light of His love. He knew when He made us that we were fragile. He wants us to depend on His strength when the tides try to pull us under. He hides us behind the rock of Jesus Christ.

The Perfect loves the imperfect. The whole loves the broken. He willingly gave up his life for this priceless collection. He loves us just the way we are, imperfect, broken and beautiful!

Thought for the Day:

Jehovah-Rapha (The Lord Who Heals) Help me to love my every imperfection. I put every broken piece of my heart at the foot of Your cross where it can be put back together and made whole.

A NEW SONG

Psalm 98:1 (NIV)

Sing to the Lord a new song, for He has done marvelous things.

One night my youngest son and his girlfriend were playing cards with my husband and me. We play cards and games together often, but this night I was feeling bored and antsy. I started to wonder what else we could do that would be more exciting. I had the great idea of going to the beach. Everyone thought I was crazy, since it was already nine o'clock at night. Shortly after ten o'clock, we were sitting on the beach eating Chinese dumplings by the light of the silvery moon.

After we finished eating, we walked along the beach. The presence of God was heavy as we began to sing praise songs. The more we sang, the more His presence increased. As we faced the thunderous ocean, the moon overwhelmed us as it cast a shimmering light across the crashing tide. A mist began to blow across our faces as we raised our hands in praise.

I felt the Lord saying that He was baptizing us with a "New Song". I looked over at my son worshipping His Father and my heart was full of joy. He looked over at me and said, "Mom, this is the best night I have ever had!"

Sometimes we have to meet God in a "new place" so that He can give us a "new song." For many of us, going to church on Sunday, reading the Bible when we can squeeze it in, and praying when we need something, is the God part of our life. Our God

7

routine is limiting Him, putting Him in a box, only letting Him out according to our schedule. He desires to change us, to grow us, and He longs to be in every facet of our lives.

When my children were growing up, I explained to them that our walk with God was like climbing a ladder. Some accept Jesus into their hearts (first rung on the ladder) and they stop there. That is as far as they choose to climb and they stay there, feeling safe. Then there are others who hunger for more. They are not content to stop at the first rung. Their climb is steady and they don't look down. They just keep looking up. They are not threatened by heights, but by complacency.

In order for us to hear the new song that God has for us, we must let Him out of the box we have put Him in and invite Him into our daily lives. Take an unexpected trip to the beach or do something you would not normally do, and expect to find Him there, waiting for you. Sing to Him a new song and don't be surprised if you hear Him sing one back to you!

Thought for the Day:

Jehovah Shammah (The Lord Is There) Forgive me for anyway I have put You in a box and become complacent. I ask for a new wind to blow through my spirit. I want more of You; help me God!

A STRAY DOG

Psalm 145:14 (NLT)

The Lord helps the fallen and lifts up those bent beneath their loads.

As I listened to her story, a picture came to mind. I was talking to one of the women in our church outreach program. Rita told me of her life and all the mistakes she had made. Her story was full of regrets, shame, and guilt. As she proceeded with her story, she told me how she and her older children were sleeping in a field. Some housing opportunities had come up here and there but she was not able to take them because she had a dog and dogs were not allowed. The first thought that came into my mind was, "Why on earth would you take in a dog when you can't even provide for yourself and your family?".

Rita began to cry as she spoke of the dog. As the tears began to flow, she quickly wiped them away and scolded herself saying, "I can't cry." When she was growing up she was taught that if you cried you were weak, and you had to stay strong. Yet she cried as she spoke of the dog saying, "The dog is just like me. When I found him he was skin and bones and had no food, water or a place to stay."

She had brought him to a place for stray dogs that would only keep him for a short while. After a few days, they would have to euthanize him if no one claimed him. When she returned, no one had taken the dog, so he would be put down. She decided to keep him; she couldn't give up on him. She said, "We brought him home and fattened him up." To Rita, giving up on that dog would be like giving up on herself. The dog was the one part of her life that made sense.

As she spoke, I began to get a picture of what God wants to do for us. Sometimes we feel just like that dog, that if someone doesn't come and claim us soon we will die. We are like stray dogs, so starving for acceptance and the affection of others that our bones are showing. Lost and alone, we long for someone to come along and tell us everything will be all right and to just love us. We ache for the sounds of family around us, for a sense of belonging, to feel warm and safe, away from the elements and the world.

I had the great honor to share the picture I saw with her as she had told me her story. I told her how Jesus wanted to do the same thing for her as she had done for the stray dog. Even through all the things she had done, He was there, waiting to claim her as His. He wanted to provide for her, give her a home, love her, and "fatten her up." He was claiming her from certain death. He would protect and cover her. They would be family and she would never be alone again. Her home was now in the shelter of His wings. Rita accepted Jesus into her heart that day.

As time passed, Rita and I stayed in contact. She began to battle brain cancer. She kept growing in the love of God through that difficult time. She would call me and say, "You always pray for me, I want to pray for you." They were the most precious, childlike prayers! I know they went straight to God's ears.

One morning the call came that Rita was in a non-responsive state, a deep, sleep. Soon Jesus would awaken her and kiss away every tear. She will never hunger or suffer pain again. Imagine always having to worry about what you will eat and where you'll sleep. Rita now has a permanent address, her Father standing at the door saying, "Welcome home, my precious daughter."

Thought for the Day:

Jehovah Jireh (Lord of Provision) Help me to not judge others. I don't know what they are going through in their lives. My earthly eyes can deceive me; help me to see others only through heavenly eyes.

ARMS WIDE OPEN

1 Corinthians 1:18 (NIV)

For the message of the cross is foolishness to those who are perishing, but to us who are being saved it is the power of God.

While preparing an Easter message, the Lord gave me a revelation that I will never forget. I saw a picture of myself standing up with my hands straight out from my sides. The Lord spoke to me in my spirit, He said, "What shape are you?" I realized that I was in the perfect shape of a cross! I am a walking, talking, blood bought, not by mistake, but purposely created in the shape of a Cross!

He showed me that when I carry things like shame, guilt, rejection, it causes me to disconnect with the power of the Cross.

The enemy of our souls comes to steal the power that is rightfully ours because of what Jesus did at Calvary.

When the enemy comes to steal, kill and destroy, we have a new weapon of warfare. All we have to do is STAND UP; arms wide open, and remind ourselves what happened that day at Calvary. We carry His Cross with us at all times; it is part of us. When we find ourselves in a troubling situation, in the deepest valleys of our lives or feeling alone, we just need to stretch out our arms wide open, and call upon the power of the cross over our lives.

What an awesome Creator we have! He is a God of detail. He even formed us in our mothers' wombs in the shape of His most precious gift. He has given us the cross, on which his very own

Son gave his life, so that we all might live. His arms were wide open as He hung on that cross with each of our names engraved in His heart.

I shared what the Lord had revealed to me while praying for a girl at our church who was full of guilt from prostitution and drug abuse. She opened her arms and realized that the body she so freely gave away was actually a reminder of the cross, which carried her shame and guilt. She smiled as a new power began filling the places where the guilt had weighed her down. Her body was no longer worthless. It had value because all she had to do was lift her arms and the power of the cross was hers.

The cross has new meaning for me now. It is so personal. I can look at my reflection in the mirror, or look at you and see the cross. It is something that no one can take from me. Someday they may take my Bible from me and tell me it is illegal for me to worship my God, but all I will have to do is open my arms and look up to heaven. The power of the cross will be mine.

It doesn't matter if we are like the homeless girl walking the streets, lost, and looking for love in all the wrong places, or like a businessman seeming to have it all together. We are all sinners, saved only by Jesus opening His arms wide and looking to His Father in heaven and saying, "It is finished." The finished work of the cross is what transpired as mercy and grace hung in our place.

Thought for the Day:

El Elyon (God Most High) Today I want to have a fresh revelation of the cross and all You have done for me through Calvary. I claim all the power that You died to give me. Let me never forget that You are as close as my arms; I lift them, and we are connected.

CLIMB EVERY MOUNTAIN

1 Corinthians15:57 (NIV)

But thanks be to God! He gives us the victory through our Lord Jesus Christ.

We all go through times when the world is an unfriendly place to live. There is no help to be found and no one seems to care that we are going through the gates of hell trying to get to the Promised Land.

Each of us has our own mountain to climb. As every experienced mountain climber will tell you, there are tricks to surviving the climb. Having had much experience climbing my own "mountains", I can share a few of my own scaling tricks with you.

First, never look down. When we do, we are concentrating on the past, and for most of us the failures come first and foremost to our minds. Failures are excess baggage that a good climber does not need. It makes us tire easily and becomes heavier the longer we carry it.

Secondly, we must learn to keep forward and upward momentum. When the storms come, we tend to retreat. We stop and turn around never to know that just a little further up the trail it was calm and the sun was shining.

Sometimes In the midst of our climb (the battle), the force of the wind makes it seem as if we will be blown away. Just like an immature tree that grows to be a strong oak, we will strengthen and grow with each storm that we endure.

From our mountain climbing experience we know that if we were to stop or fall down now, it would take twice the energy and strength to pull ourselves up and get going again. The only way we will know the power we have inside of us is to keep putting one foot in front of the other. The driving force that pushes us forward even when we feel we can't go another step is not an earthly power but that of the Spirit that lives within.

Finally, we will reach the top of our mountain and plant the flag that has "Victory" imprinted on it! The mountain, which once loomed before us as unconquerable, is under our feet.

As we begin our descent, the wind is at our backs. The journey is effortless compared to the long and arduous uphill climb. The winds that tried to stop us are now blowing us to our destination.

Keep walking, don't look down, and don't stop no matter how hard the winds blow. Know that you are not walking alone. The Spirit living inside of you is with you and just waiting to shout, "Victory is ours" with just a few more steps!

Thought for the Day:

Jehovah-Sabaoth (Lord Of The Armies) When I am in the valley, help me to know You are guiding me up the mountain, and that You are the wind at my back.

DEEPER WATERS

Matthew 14:29 (NLT)

"Yes, come" Jesus said. So Peter went over the side of the boat and walked on the water toward Jesus.

There are times in our lives, like Peter, we are asked to come out of our boat (our comfort zone) and walk on the water (unfamiliar territory). When I think about Peter on the boat and Jesus saying, "Yes, come," I wonder what I would have done. Having almost drowned twice, I don't have to wonder long at what my response would have been. The past has a way of coming back and reminding us of what happened last time. For most of my life, I would only swim in water where my feet could touch the bottom and the water was not over my head.

One day, as I was journaling to the Lord, I heard in my Spirit that He wanted to bring me out to deeper waters. He said that it would be over my head but that I wouldn't even get wet. He was challenging me to take the plunge and trust Him.

Matthew 14:29-30 (NIV) goes on to say, *"Then Peter got down out of the boat, walked on the water and came toward Jesus. But when he saw the wind he was afraid and beginning to sink, cried out, "Lord, save me!"*

When Peter first started walking on the water, he had his eyes fixed on Jesus. When he took his eyes off Jesus he changed his focus. Suddenly he saw the world, the water, the wind, and his vulnerability. He began to sink as his faith sank. Peter's faith was strong enough to heed the call but not yet strong enough to walk all the way to where Jesus stood.

For each of us, our call to walk on the water will be different. My own experience will not be like yours, but I know from following Him that He will never leave us in the boat. He will always challenge us to step out into the waters of uncertainty. It is there in the midst of waves and turbulence that we learn to trust the One who controls the water.

Thought for the Day:

Jehovah-Shammah (The Lord Is My Companion) Help me to hear Your voice calling me to come out into the deep, and give me the faith and courage to walk on the water and meet You.

WHO AM I?

Ephesians 2:10 (NLT)

For we are God's masterpiece, He has created us anew in Christ Jesus, so we can do the good things he planned for us long ago.

When I first saw this scripture, I loved it, and personalized it; for I am God's masterpiece; He created me anew in Christ Jesus. I spoke it out loud and then I spoke it again. I felt empowered by the words. I never thought of myself as a masterpiece! I pictured an artist being so intimate with his painting, a laborious work, something created from deep within his soul; hours, days, even years spent on this masterpiece. The finished product is unlike any other, special, created with love and purpose.

I think we would all love to change something about ourselves. We are familiar with every flaw. We could give a long request list. We would argue with our Creator "Why did I have to be so short, so tall, so…?"

We are shaped by the opinions of those by whom we are surrounded, our parents, family, teachers, and friends. Our childhood has a lot to do with whom we believe we are. I was made fun of as a child, as everyone was, but it is much different today. Bullying is out of control to the point that teen suicide is at an all-time high.

Our Creator is in love with His creation. He even gave us individual fingerprints, one of a kind. He wouldn't change one thing about us. His heart loves our heart. This scripture says that he created us in Christ Jesus, to do the things he planned for us long ago. A destiny was affixed to our creation. You are not a mistake. Love, purpose, destiny were all combined to make you.

One day I was at the mall and needed help with some skin care products. I didn't see anyone working at the counter at first, but in a short while a woman came out from the back room and walked towards me. God did something to me that I had never experienced before. It is hard to explain, but He changed my eyes as if I were looking through His eyes. All I could see as I looked at the woman behind the counter was beauty, indescribable, heavenly beauty. As I began to speak, the words "You are so beautiful" just spilled out of my mouth. At first I was embarrassed, I didn't even know who she was, but then I noticed she was crying. We were hugging before I knew it, and I could feel the Presence of God right there in the middle of a department store. She shared with me that she had been feeling depressed, her husband had cheated on her and left her. God knew that she needed to know how beautiful she was, and he let me see how beautiful she was to Him. That's all that really matters, isn't it, that the one who created us sees us as his beautiful masterpiece?

Thought for the Day:

Jehovah-Elroi (The God Who Sees Me) Help me to know who I am in You Lord. You created me intentionally, with a destiny. I was not a mistake. Your eyes only see my beauty; I am Your masterpiece, created in Christ Jesus!

EARLY SUNRISE

Matt. 5:14-15 (NLT)

You are the light of the world-like a city on a mountain, glowing in the night for all to see. Don't hide your light under a basket! Instead, put it on a stand and let it shine for all.

As I pull back the curtains from my hotel room, I am reminded of how beautiful the sunrise is at the beach. It's early, too early for most to be awake. Not wanting to miss the beauty of the sunrise, I forego the chance to sleep in and perhaps dream of one instead. The sound of the crashing waves is the only distraction from the serenity of a landscape uninhibited by man.

I believe that God lives at the beach, He seems so easy to find when I go there. The quiet and peace is contagious and is a conduit to hearing His voice and feeling His presence.

As I watch the transformation of the sunrise above the clouds, a common thread comes to mind. For some of us, the clouds of past failures, and broken relationships cover us. Inside of all of us is a sun waiting to rise, but it is covered by the darkness of our past.

We hold onto that cloud. We've gotten used to the feeling of its covering, protecting us from anyone seeing the real us. We wake up in the morning, put on our cloud of protection and off we go. The thing we don't realize is that as that cloud is being put on we are snuffing out the light of Jesus that burns within us. He

19

wants us to rise above the clouds and be so bright that wherever we go we dispel the darkness. Rather than hiding our past failures, he wants us to give them to Him so our light is not hidden.

One day I felt the Lord was showing me a picture of someone sitting in a dark cave. They were desperately looking for just a crack of light, a ray of hope. Even the tiniest crack would mean there was a chance of escape. How many people are sitting in darkness, afraid and alone, desperately looking for that one ray of hope? We are to be the light of hope to a dark, troubled world, trapped in darkness.

Watching the sun break through the darkness is a reminder that every morning is new, and brings with it another sunrise and another chance to begin again.

Lamentations 3:22 (NIV) *Because of the Lord's great love we are not consumed for his compassions never fail. They are new every morning; great is your faithfulness.*

Thought for the Day:

Adonai (My Great Lord) Help me to be Your light in a dark world today.

SEEKING THE PRESENCE

Hebrews 11:27 (NLT)

It was by faith that Moses left the land of Egypt, not fearing the king's anger. He kept right on going because he kept his eyes on the one who is invisible.

M oses kept his eyes on the one who is invisible. How can we keep our eyes on someone who is invisible? Reflecting on Moses life according to God's Word will help us to get an answer to this question.

The following is an encapsulated version of the relationship and experiences between God and Moses. We are all familiar with the story of God speaking to Moses through a burning bush. That definitely got Moses attention!

Deuteronomy 10:10 informs us that Moses stayed on the mountain in the Lord's presence for forty days and nights. In Exodus 33:11 we are told that the Lord spoke to Moses face to face as a man speaks to his friend. They had history together. God sought out Moses, trusted him, and called him friend. God asked Moses to do many things that challenged him. He stuttered yet God wanted him to go to Pharaoh, the highest power in the land and speak to him about setting the Israelites free. He is then asked to lead about two million people through a desert, a journey that ended up lasting forty years. God spoke to him through a thick cloud during those forty years. God asked Moses to perform some very challenging tasks. He said yes. He would do whatever his friend God asked him to do no matter how daunting a task it was, no matter how far out of his comfort zone it was.

God talked to Moses because they had a relationship. Moses could keep his eyes on the One who is invisible because he was so used to being in the Presence of God. His whole life was a dedication to God. He would go anywhere, leave his home, and even trek through a desert for forty years because all he desired was to follow the Presence. Whether it was a cloud, a flaming bush, or spending forty days on a mountain top with his trusted friend, as the scripture says: he kept right on going, always needing God's presence to guide, direct and lead him to the next encounter with God.

How does God speak to you? The Word says, "My sheep hear my voice." Are you willing to do anything, give up everything to follow the Presence? Do you consider God your friend? Are you willing to be pushed out of your "comfort zone" to find the place of Presence? Moses paid a price in the natural (giving up riches, his home, spending forty years in the desert) to receive the spiritual. Are you willing to give up all that you have in the natural to receive all that you were truly created for by God? Keep going, press in, desperately searching, and be determined to set your eyes on the invisible God now made visible to you by His Presence.

Thought for the Day:

Jehovah-Nissi (The Lord Is My Banner) Place a hunger in me for Your Presence. Such a hunger that I would be willing to give up all of my worldly desires in search of You. I want to hear You call me Your friend. Help me to say yes to whatever You are calling me to do.

FACE TO FACE

Exodus 33:11 (NIV)

The Lord would speak to Moses face to face, as a man speaks with his friend.

As far as our communication has come, we still cannot see our Heavenly Father face to face. We talk to Him through prayer. For some, it is hard to talk with someone they can't see. They don't even try because they don't believe that anyone is listening. Yet in 1 Peter 3:12 it says, *"For the eyes of the Lord are on the righteous and his ears are attentive to their prayer."* Not only is He listening, but also you will see, as we look closely at the next scripture, how much He is treasuring our prayers!

In Revelation 5:8b it says, *"Each one (the* four living creatures and the twenty four elders Rev. 5:8a) *had a harp and they were holding golden bowls full of incense which are the prayers of the saints."* Imagine our prayers in golden bowls! God not only hears them but He saves them. They are that important to Him!

It reminds me of saving flowers from someone we love and drying them so they keep forever. Somehow we can't throw them away because they remind us of someone who means so much to us. Saving a favorite card from a loved one is the same. Every once in a while we read it again and it connects and reminds us of our loved one. Could it be that our prayers are so valuable to our Heavenly Father that he just has to save them until we see each other face to face?

Gold has always been a symbol of great value. The fact that our prayers are in gold bowls speaks of how priceless they are. They are a sacrifice, a valuable gift to Him.

The Word says that our prayers are incense to God. In the Old Testament, incense was burned and offered as a sacrifice to God. In Exodus 30:8, the Lord gave Moses instruction for Aaron to burn fragrant incense on the altar every morning and again at twilight so incense would burn regularly before Him.

1 Thessalonians 5:17 urges us to pray without ceasing. We should send our prayers up to Him constantly, just as Aaron continually sent up the sweet aroma of incense. He loves the sweet smell of consistent prayer. Yes, our prayers have a fragrant odor! In Psalm 141:2 David appeals to the Lord *"May my prayer be set before you like incense."*

When you pray, close your eyes and picture your prayers going straight up to your Father. Visualize him breathing in the sweet fragrance of your prayers and saving them in a golden bowl until you meet Him face to face!

Thought for the Day:

Jehovah-Shammah (the Lord is there) I am so thankful that my prayers pass through the heavens and reach You. May they be a sweet fragrance to You.

FOLLOW ME

Matthew 4:19 (KJV)

And he saith unto them, Follow me, and I will make you fishers of men."

When I started to meditate on this passage of scripture, I tried to put myself in the place of Simon, later called Peter, and his brother Andrew. There they were, fishing with their nets, something they had done day after day for many years, when Jesus called out to them.

Picture yourself at work doing what you usually do and in walks this man that you have never seen before. He says to you, "Drop everything you are doing, leave your families and follow me. I am going to change everything you have known, maybe even your name, everything familiar, shake your sense of security, and make you a fisher of men!"

I don't think for one second that either Simon Peter or Andrew had any idea what Jesus meant by becoming "a fisher of men." Yet as I read on it says in verse twenty, they left their nets at once, and went with him.

Verse twenty-one and twenty two of Matthew 4 (NLT) says "A little farther up the shore Jesus saw two other brothers, James and John sitting in a boat with their father, Zebedee, repairing their nets." And He called them to come, too. Verse 22 says, "They immediately followed him, leaving the boat and their father behind."

In Matthew 8:19-20 (NIV) we learn about the cost of following Jesus. A teacher of religious law tells Jesus he will follow Him no matter where He goes. Jesus' answer is "Foxes have dens, birds have nests, but the Son of Man has no place to lay his head." Jesus was saying, "Perhaps you should consider the bigger picture."

In Matthew 19:20, a rich young man seeking eternal life tells Jesus he has kept all the commandments then asks "What else must I do? Jesus tells him to sell what he has and give to the poor. At this, the man turns away, pockets full; he can't let go of his world. Think of someone who has attained great success by today's standards. How hard would it be for them to relinquish all they had worked for, give it to the poor and not look back?

Jesus is still searching for disciples to leave everything they have and follow Him. It sometimes involves leaving jobs, families, even our homes.

Ten years ago, the Lord called me to leave my job, my health insurance, and my security, and take a volunteer ministry position. It was a time of growth for me, learning to do without many things of the "world" and to trust that He would provide. There were times I thought about returning to the job market (the thought of a regular paycheck can be enticing). Looking back, there is no price that could replace the memories of all the people I have met and helped through the years.

How many today are willing to answer the call to become a disciple of Jesus, ready to leave the comforts of which we have become so accustomed, to drop our nets and become fishers of men? Jesus is still looking and asking us the same question he asked the fishermen, "Will you come and follow Me?"

Thought for the Day:

Jehovah-Rohi (The Lord Is My Shepherd) I want to be ready to follow You at any cost. I pray that I would answer Your call as quickly as the disciples did. Prepare my heart and make me the disciple You have called me to be.

GOD OF CREATION

Genesis 1:1-2 (NLT)

In the beginning God created the heavens and the earth. The earth was empty, a formless mass cloaked in darkness. And the Spirit of God was hovering over the surface.

I love that word "hovering". I can just close my eyes and picture the Spirit of God hovering over a vast expanse of emptiness. It is like an artist looking at a blank canvas and envisioning what it would be like if it was filled with the color and movement of life.

The day we are born, our blank canvas begins to fill with experiences. Our life's journey will have some dark clouds, sunny skies, laughter, and tears. Looking back on my canvas I see times in my life where I felt I was walking alone, but all the time the Holy Spirit was hovering over me. He has never left me or forsaken me. We are the natural born artists of our own lives. I have trouble drawing stick people, yet I hold in my hand the paintbrush of an accomplished artist. I have the choice to paint a beautiful landscape for the world to gaze at or paint a picture of pain and regrets.

When we receive the news that we are to have a baby, we usually begin the process of preparing for the new arrival. We paint the room, fill it with brightly colored toys and mobiles, we wouldn't think of putting our new addition in a blank room, cold and lifeless.

Jesus painted our room with a beautiful azure sky, billowing clouds, luscious shades of green trees and plants, and diamond-like stars to gaze upon day and night. There are flowers of every color that we can smell and take in the sweet fragrance, a bouquet given to us by our Abba Father.

Man was made on the last day of creation. Everything had to be in place before He introduced His precious children their new home. He placed Adam and Eve in the Garden of Eden. It is hard to imagine how beautiful that must have been.

Genesis 1:27 declares that we are made in God's image. Since we are made in His image, it means that creativity was born into us. We have the ability to create what our life will be. We can choose to conform to the world's image of who we are, or we can choose to conform to our Godly image. Anything in us that does not resemble God is a counterfeit and we have the choice to accept or reject it.

One day we will all stand before Christ, carrying our self-portrait in our hand. The canvas that started as blank and lifeless is now filled with varying shades and depths of colors, expressed by the intensity of experiences we have walked through. We will present it to the God of Creation, He who has been hovering over us on our journey. What will your canvas look like?

Thought for the Day:

Elohim (Creator) As I pick up the paintbrush of my life, I choose to paint my canvas with colors of forgiveness, beauty, joy and love.

GRUMBLING AND UNBELIEF

Numbers 14:28 (NIV)

So tell them, 'As surely as I live, declares the Lord I will do to you the very things I heard you say.' I, the Lord, have spoken!

When I look closely at this verse in scripture, two things immediately come to mind. The first is that God hears EVERYTHING we say. That is a little scary to think about. The second is how much power our words possess. Proverbs 18:21 states "Death and life are in the power of the tongue."

In Numbers 14:2 (GW), all the Israelites grumbled against Moses and Aaron, and the whole assembly and said to them, "If only we had died in Egypt! Or in this desert!"

The Israelites brought punishment upon themselves just by what they spoke out of their mouths. They said they would rather die in the desert than to go into Canaan, and die they did. The number of Jews included in the exodus from Egypt is estimated to be at anywhere from 600,000 to 3 million! Sadly, only two of the original group, Joshua and Caleb, ever got to see the Promised Land. I wonder how many of God's blessings we miss because we kill them with our own words.

One day a lady came into our ministry and asked if I knew where she could get a walker. I was puzzled by the request because she walked perfectly well. When I asked her why, she said she had an appointment to file a Social Security Disability claim. She wanted to walk in with a walker in order to enhance her chances of getting disability. I was upset and reminded her how dishonest it was. She didn't come back for quite some time. When she did I did not recognize her. She could hardly stand on her own; she was walking with a walker! She had lost half her weight and had aged considerably. God hears our every word, our every request.

In the past I worked in a nursing home. It was divided into different floors depending on level of care. I worked on the Alzheimer's floor. One day, I was walking some of my patients past the fully cognitive, elite section of the nursing home. I still remember one lady looking with great disdain and murmuring to another lady about my patients. She even told me that they should stay on their own floor. One day soon after, while at work on my floor, I looked down the hallway and to my surprise a nurse was pushing a wheelchair with that same lady in it. She remained on our Alzheimer's floor until she died. God hears our murmurings.

But the wonderful part about all of this is that God also hears our words of faith, praise, and thanks. The Bible is full of His life words and He responds to ours. When we speak from the Book of Life He has given us, we can expect to make it to the Land of Milk and Honey. We will not perish in the desert.

God's desire was for all of his people to enter the Promised Land. Joshua and Caleb refused to take their eyes off the promises of God. No matter how it looked in the natural, they kept their spiritual eyes opened and refused to join the crowd filled with complainers and non-believers. There were great odds against them yet they held fast continuing to walk and talk in faith.

With all the fear and worry in the world today, it is easy to fall prey to the negative. The odds are against us too. With bankruptcy, foreclosure, cancer at an all time high, and uncertainty in our leadership, we must be the Joshuas and Calebs of our times! We must let our words be the passport to our Promised Land!

Thought for the Day:

El Shaddai (All Sufficient One) Let the words of my mouth be pleasing to You today. I repent for every murmur, every complaint, and every word I have spoken that was displeasing to Your ears. I give You this day and rejoice in it because this is the day that You have made!

GUARDING OUR HEARTS

Proverbs 4:23 (NIV)

Above all else, guard your heart for it is the wellspring of life.

In my prayer time the Lord showed me a picture of a heart. The words "Heart Attack" were written across it. I wasn't sure what He was trying to tell me so I went to my computer and looked up heart attack. According to The National Heart Lung and Blood Institute, a heart attack occurs if the flow of oxygen-rich blood to a section of heart muscle suddenly becomes blocked. If the blood flow isn't restored quickly, the section of the heart muscle begins to die. The dead heart muscle is replaced with scar tissue.

The Lord then showed me that we could also have a spiritual heart attack. Just as the supply of blood and oxygen is cut off in a physical heart attack, the supply of spiritual blood (the Blood of the Lamb) and the oxygen (the Breath of the Holy Spirit) can also be cut off.

Even as death occurs to the muscle in a physical heart attack, death to our spiritual hearts can cause our hearts to be lifeless. Webster's Dictionary defines the heart as the core of our being, the center of our emotions and innermost thoughts. Trauma, hurt, abuse, neglect, and sin can cause us to have a heart that beats but has no life.

Just as we receive scar tissue from a physical heart attack, we can also have emotional scarring from the hurts we receive. One of the definitions for a scar is the lasting mental or emotional effect of suffering.

If we could look deep into our hearts we would probably see many scars, and also discover that the wound underneath the scar has never been healed. Bitterness and unforgiveness cause our hearts to harden and, by choosing not to forgive, we allow the enemy to claim that part of our heart as his territory.

In the Spirit, The Lord showed me a picture of my heart. I had much unforgiveness. There was a part of my heart that had army trucks riding across it. It was owned by the devil. He was squatting on the land of my heart, and taking ownership. The enemy of my heart knew that if I forgave all those whom had hurt me, and I released my judgment from them, he would no longer have a legal right to stay there. He dwells where there is death, God dwells where there is life. With my acts of forgiveness God would regain the areas of my heart that had suffered the heart attack.

The words of Deuteronomy 30:6 (NLT) declare, *"The Lord your God will change your heart and the hearts of all your descendants, so that you will love him with all your heart and soul and so you may live!"*

In Ezekiel 36:26 (AMP) it says, "*And I will give you a new heart with new and right desires, and I will put a new spirit in you. I will take out your stony heart of sin and give you a new obedient heart.*"

When someone has a physical heart attack statistics say if you get to an emergency room right away, and have CPR (Cardiopulmonary Resuscitation) the survival rate is very high. God also has CPR for our spiritual hearts.

C - Claim the healing that Jesus died to give you.

P - Possess the land of your heart. You must take back rightful ownership.

R - Release those you have held in judgment and unforgiveness.

The Good News is that the statistics for survival using God's CPR is one hundred percent! As we go to God's "Emergency Room" He will breathe life into the areas once pronounced dead. His blood will now be able to flow freely and every blockage will be removed. We can now praise Him with a whole heart!

Psalm 86:12 (NLT) "*With ALL my heart I will praise you O Lord My God!*"

Thought for the Day:

Jehovah Rapha (The Lord Who Heals) I give You my heart.
Blow the wind of Your Spirit into every dry place and let Your water of life flow through, healing every scar from the inside out.

HOLY EXPECTATIONS

Psalm 62:5 (ASV)

My soul waits thou in silence for God only; for my expectation is from him.

I was on vacation last week and I got to spend some quality time with God. In my quiet time with the Lord I heard the words "unholy expectations", in other words, I had subscribed to wrong thoughts and beliefs. I asked Him to show me what those wrong thoughts and beliefs were. He brought to my mind times in the past that everything seemed to be going well and it would make me nervous. I would be waiting for the proverbial other shoe to drop. The better things got the more nervous I became. My mind had developed a pattern that said watch out; something bad is bound to happen.

That is exactly where the enemy wants to keep us. Stuck in a place that says nothing is ever going to change; that this is as good as it gets. He reminds us of all of our shortcomings and ridicules our courage to think bigger or have higher expectations.

In John 10:10 (NIV) we are warned, *"The thief comes only to steal and kill and destroy; I have come that they may have life, and have it to the full."*

When the ravaging winds of life blow our way, we must run as fast as we can to our most trusted advisor, the Word of God. We must see if the decisions we are making line up with the Word or with the enemy and then check our expectations. Are they holy or unholy? Are we letting fear, doubt and worry guide our decision? Once those spirits gain control of us we are out of the realm of faith. Faith is belief in what we cannot see. If we are looking at our situation from an earthly perspective we are looking through clouded glasses. God uses situations to stretch our faith. Will we be found faithful?

Thought for the Day:

Jehovah-Nissi (The Lord Is My Banner) Help me today to look at every situation, good or bad, with eyes that have been fixed on You and Your Word. I choose to remove the glasses that cloud my vision and put on the glasses of faith.

I SPEAK LIFE

Isaiah 38:18 (NLT)

For the dead cannot praise you; they cannot raise their voices in praise. Those who go down to destruction can no longer hope in your faithfulness.

I received my juror notice in the mail. I didn't pay too much attention to it. Usually when I receive a call to jury duty, I call and they tell me I don't have to come in. This time, however it was different. I did need to report, and little did I know that the next three days would change my life.

I was not expecting to do the deep soul searching that transpired in those three days. I was a candidate to possibly become a juror on a double murder trial. A questionnaire was handed out to the one hundred potential jurors. It was nineteen pages long, and focused on whether or not we believed in the death penalty.

I must say that until this time I had never really made a firm decision on my beliefs about this subject, mostly because I never had to. And now, I was suddenly hit head on with making a decision about life and death.

The first day the prosecuting attorney, defense attorney, and the judge interviewed each of us. They asked if we had any reasons for not being able to be a juror, and especially if we could vote yea on the death penalty if required.

During the questioning I noticed a man looking directly at us. It was the man who would be tried for the murders. As I looked at him, I began to realize the responsibility that God had placed in my hands. When I got home that night, I began to weep and ask God what I should do. I wanted to know what His thoughts were. I asked Him to show me in His Word. I immediately heard "Thou shall not kill." Then in my spirit I heard myself talking to the homeless at my church where my husband and I taught on Sunday mornings. I heard myself telling them "No matter what you have done, if you genuinely repent and ask forgiveness, the Lord will not remember it. You will be forgiven."

Isaiah 43:25 (NIV) encourages us with God's own words "*I, even I, am he who blots out your transgressions, for my own sake, and remembers your sin no more."* How could I make a decision to have someone put to death and yet speak those words every Sunday?

I went one step further. I asked God to give me a dream, a confirmation. I woke up the next morning with the memory of a dream vividly in my mind. In the dream I was at an unfamiliar house with a crowd of strangers. One of the men was holding a baby. He turned suddenly and threw the baby at me. I was startled and almost dropped it.

I told my husband of the dream. He said a baby represents life. I felt the Lord was saying that we are sometimes so careless with life. The man in my dream just threw the baby (life) at me not caring what would happen to it. The most wonderful thing God showed me through the dream was how much He cares about life. He is the one who created it, and He gets upset when it is not valued.

As long as we have breath, we have he ability to praise God. As long as we have breath we have the ability to speak to others about His unconditional love. We can tell those on death row that there is someone who loves them, and if they truly repent and yes to God, he will blow the wind of His Spirit into them and death will be no more.

Thought for the Day:

Jehovah-Shalom (The Lord Is Peace) Thank You for Your breath of life. I want to breathe You in, fill me to overflowing. If there is anything in me that is not connected to life, remove it God. You are Life, I am made in Your image, make me like You.

IDENTITY THEFT

John 8:24 (NIV)

"I told you that you would die in your sins; if you do not believe that I am the one I claim to be, you will indeed die in your sins."

Jesus was talking to the Pharisees and the Jews in this scripture. He is also talking to us. We have to believe who He is otherwise our sins will be buried with us when we die. We must also know who we are in Christ.

Satan questioned Jesus as to who He was and tried to get Him to doubt His own authority by saying in Matthew 4:3 *" If you are the Son of God tell these stones to become bread."* In Matthew 4:5-6, then the devil took Him to the holy city and had Him stand on the highest point of the temple. *"If you are the Son of God,"* he said, *"throw yourself down."*

Just as Satan questioned Jesus he will also try to make us question our identity. It started with Adam and Eve in the garden. Before the infamous "bite of the apple" Adam and Eve were pure. Of course Satan had a problem with God's latest creation; mankind would be a reflection of God himself! So Satan devised a plan to corrupt the human race. He is still having a problem with our identity as sons and daughters of the Most High God. He starts trying to distort our belief of who God is and who we are as soon as we are born. He hates that he was thrown down from heaven, and he despises everyone connected to the great God, Jehovah, the ultimate bouncer of heaven.

Today's world is filled with identity theft. With so much social media, networking, computers, tablets and mobile phones, it is much easier to for identities to become compromised. While most people know about identity theft in the world, they don't realize that there is another thief. His name is Satan. One of his jobs is to steal our identity in Christ. Jesus warns us in John 10:10 (NIV) *"The thief comes only to steal, kill and destroy."* Satan says we are doomed as sinners, that what we have done can never be forgiven. God declares us righteous when we repent for our sins. Satan says we get our identity through what we've done. God says our identity comes from what He has done. Romans 8:1-2 tells us we are free forever from condemnation.

It is up to us to choose whose words we will believe. That choice was given to us at a high cost. The blood that was shed for our identity does not change or lose its power. Therefore, the truth of our identity never changes. God identifies us as His, so we must reject the enemy's lies. Choose today to walk in freedom, having no doubt, knowing that you are God's creation. Nothing of the enemy, the world, society, friends, family, or any of the things of man can dictate who you are. Be set free today.

Thought for the Day:

Jehovah-El-Roi (The God Who Sees Me) Forgive me for any time I have believed the lies of the enemy and allowed him to rob me of my identity in You. Thank you for the blood You shed to give me my true identity as a child of the Most High God.

JOURNEY OF LOVE

Hebrews 13:1-2 (NLT)

Continue to love each other with true Christian love. Don't forget to show hospitality to strangers, for some who have done this have entertained angels without realizing it!

I was feeling homesick as I surveyed the azure sky above me. It was a balmy day in Zambia, Africa. I was there on a mission trip. It was Sunday and we were to visit one of the churches built by missionaries who had been there before us. After a two-hour drive on bumpy terrain, careening from side to side amidst jutting rocks and potholes, we parked our car and began our mile long hike into the bush.

Once our feet hit the ground we were greeted by a myriad of buttery smooth, ebony skinned little smiling faces. In every direction we looked there seemed to be little children. Even though we did not speak the same language, there was a communication between us that did not require words. There was a little girl who was about six years old, fixing her bright cinnamon colored eyes to mine. I smiled at her and she immediately took hold of my hand and never let go. I felt such an aching in her for the love of a mother. She captured my heart and I will never be the same.

We walked together down the well-traveled, dusty road, our shadows following us. The sandy, parched soil engulfed our temporary footprints, her little footsteps right beside mine. Once in a while I would hear rustling in the bushes and another child would peep his head out and join us as we walked.

I began to worry about the little girl's family. I wondered why they were not looking for her, checking to see where she was. How different life was here compared to back home. I turned to one of the local pastors who walked with us, expressing my concern about the little girl's family. She had been with me all day. He explained to me that most of the children's parents had died from AIDS. Many of the young children were trying to raise their even younger brothers and sisters. Sadly, there was no one that would be worrying about my new little friend.

The time came to say goodbye. It was bittersweet. I was so thankful that God had given me the privilege of giving His love to this little angel and at the same time tearful to know our paths would not cross again until we meet again in heavenly places. I left a part of my heart on that dusty road that day. It was a momentary journey of love, yet one that will remain in my heart forever.

Thought for the Day:

Adonai (My Great Lord) Give me a hunger to think beyond my own horizons today. Stretch my prayers to reach to places I may never go, for people I will never meet in person. Open my heart and mind to pray for those Your heart is breaking for, the widow, the unwashed and unwanted, the orphan who has lost their family due to AIDS. Give me a piece of your heart that lets me feel compassion for the least of these.

LAST CALL

Matthew 24:30-31 (NLT)

And then at last, the sign of the coming of the Son of Man will appear in the heavens, and there will be deep mourning among all the nations of the earth. And they will see the Son of Man arrive on the clouds of heaven with power and great glory. And he will send forth his angels with the sound of a mighty trumpet blast, and they will gather together his chosen ones from the farthest ends of the earth and heaven.

I was journaling, listening to what The Lord was speaking to my Spirit. He said, "I need you to make a 'Last Call'." I am coming soon and I need my people to announce loud and clear, "Last Call."

When I met my husband, he was the keyboard player in the band at my class reunion. I love music, and especially loved the music his band played. I fell in love with the keyboard player who became my husband.

In the early years of our marriage, I would accompany him as he performed at different venues. In the beginning, it was mostly nightclub work. One thing that all the clubs had in common was the "Last Call." You had one last chance to buy a drink before the bar was closed. It was shouted very loudly to make sure everyone heard it.

In Genesis 7 we learn what happened after Noah, his family and the animals had boarded the ark. Verse 16 says, *"Then the Lord shut them in."* Once the door was shut, the world missed its "Last Call."

John 20:30 speaks of our Savior's crucifixion. With his last breath, Jesus said *"It is finished."* Those words penetrated the air and proclaimed that something momentous had just occurred. It was the last call for the enemy, who would no longer have rule and reign over God's children. He closed and locked the door of sin behind with the key of victory.

In Genesis 19:26, God sent angels to Sodom and Gomorrah with His "Last Call" message. Lot and his family were the only ones to escape the fire and brimstone God's wrath. They heard God's last call and were on their way to safety. Rescue was eminent. The only command given them was to not look back. Lot's wife didn't heed God's last call and was turned into a pillar of salt. People today can still hear the last call, but sometimes choose to look back for a taste of their old ways. That decision can prove to be fatal, just as it was for Lot's wife. When we take our eyes off of God to look back on the things of this world, we can easily lose sight of His path for us.

People have been drinking the wine of the world for so long that they have no idea that time is running out. They are unaware that Psalm 75:8 (NLT) says; *"For The Lord holds a cup in his hand; it is full of foaming wine mixed with spices. He pours the wine out in judgment, and all the wicked must drink it, draining it to the dregs."* This is the cup of God's wrath.

The wine of the world is hypnotizing. It "helps" us forget our troubles for a time. But when we sober up our problems are still there. The next time problems overtake us; we drink from the same cup of seduction. Time is ticking away, and that the door could close at any moment.

However, we can stay in communion with God and drink from the cup of His salvation. Jesus has offered the cup of grace and mercy. Will you accept this invitation purchased with His shed blood? We have to choose from which cup we will drink.
Last Call!

Thought for the Day:
Jehovah-Sabaoth (The Lord Of Armies) Make me Your voice in a world that has shut its ears to the things of God. Put urgency in my spirit to speak boldly in faith so that deaf ears will open and blind eyes will see the coming of the Lord. Prepare our hearts to receive all that You died to give us on Calvary.

LEARNING TO TRUST

Isaiah 2:22 (NIV)

Stop trusting in man, who has but a breath in his nostrils. Of what account is he?

I was helping in a ministry where some of us were asked our opinion about an important decision which was to be made. After praying and seeking the Lord, I gave an answer, which turned out to be totally opposite to what others had heard.

I was made to feel as though I heard wrong and was off the mark. I remember not being able to sleep that night because I questioned whether anything I heard from God was right. How could I have been so sure yet so wrong? It really threw me for a loop. I began my usual devotions when I came across the above scripture. Was I going to trust man or God? It hit home.

As it turned out, the following day there was quite a turnaround. The answer had come for the circumstance for which we had all been praying. It was in agreement with the answer God had given me. This was an eye opening experience for me. Sometimes we think because someone seems more spiritual or has a higher position in the church that they are hearing from God and we must have heard wrong... But who is man that has but breath in his nostrils?

The enemy of our souls hates it when we communicate with our Father. He knows that he is in trouble when we have the confidence that we are truly hearing from "The Source". Satan works desperately to make us think that it is our own thoughts and not our Father that we are hearing. Both our communication and relationship with God are very dangerous for the devil because when we talk to God every day, we become familiar with the voice of our Father.

The more we study our bible, the more we learn the heart and thoughts of God. 2 Corinthians 10:5 instructs us to take every thought captive. It took me a while to really understand the meaning of that. The word "every" is a very strong word. My husband and I tried to take every thought captive for one day. It was a hard job.

Looking up the word "captive" in the Thesaurus is quite interesting. Some words of comparison are imprisoned, caged, attentive, and ensnared. The definition of captive in Webster's dictionary is prisoner, unable to escape. We must take our words and thoughts prisoner or they will imprison us. We must be attentive to them because they reveal what is in our hearts. When we are taking our thoughts and words captive, we are not just letting them run wild with no concern for the consequences, we are taking responsibility for them. Once taking every thought captive becomes a habit, we will have better discernment regarding who is speaking. Is it our thoughts; God's thoughts, or the enemy's thoughts? Our trust in our own hearing will grow as our discernment grows.

When we know that our Father is speaking to our spirit, He becomes alive to us and we can ask questions expecting to hear answers. Man's opinion suddenly has no effect on us; after all, man has but breath in his nostrils!

Hebrews 13:6 (NLT) declares, "So *we can say with confidence, "The Lord is my helper, so I will have no fear. What can mere people do to me?"*

Thought for the Day:

Elohim (Creator) Let Your thoughts be my thoughts. I bind my mind to the mind of Christ. I pray my words will be pleasing to Your ears today.

LEARNING TO WALK

Mark 2:11 (NIV)

I tell you, get up, take your mat and walk.

I remember when my son began trying to walk. He would go a few steps and fall, sometimes skinning his knee, or the fall would scare him and he would cry. I would run and pick him up and reassure him everything was okay.

One day a friend came by with her son, who was about the same age as mine. As we watched them play together, I couldn't help but notice how well her son was walking. That day, when my son fell, I ran and picked him up. My friend commented, "He is never going to learn if you keep picking him up. He has to learn to pick himself up. It will make his legs stronger and his balance better." She was right, I took her advice and in no time my son was not just walking but running!

Sometimes as parents, we have to watch our children fall even though we could pick them up and make everything better. I think God is the same way with us. He has to watch us fall just as I had to watch my son. He knows we will develop strength from picking ourselves back up; we will become stronger and be running in no time.

One day while driving home from work, I saw a young girl sitting on the sidewalk crying. I immediately stepped on the brakes, pulled over, put my car in park, ready to jump out and rescue the girl. In my spirit I heard God say, "Did I tell you to do that?" I said, "No, but I thought you wanted us to help people." He said, "I have another plan for her. You would be interfering with my plan." I put my car back in drive and off I went. I learned a valuable lesson that day. There are times in our life when we need to be rescued and times when we need to be left alone to pick ourselves back up and strengthen our legs so we don't fall so hard the next time.

I remember times in my life when I cried out to God and said, "Are you there? Do you see me down here; don't you see what I am going through? Did you forget about me?" Looking back, I now realize that through those hard times, He was always there, but he was teaching me how to walk, fall and pick myself back up. He wanted my legs to become strong enough to be able to run to Him.

Thought for the Day:

Jehovah-El-Roi (The God Who Sees) Thank You for always being there for me. Whether You pick me up or tell me to pick up my mat and walk, You are there, my faithful, loving Father.

THOU SHALL LOVE THY NEIGHBOR

John 15:21 (NIV)

They will treat you this way because of my name, for they do not know the One who sent me.

When we really get to know someone, that person begins to share things that have happened in their life. Eventually they will mention someone that hurt them very badly. Whether it is family or friend, I think we have all had some memories we would rather forget. It would be much easier to live without them. Abusive parents cause much havoc in people's lives, as do other family members, past or present boyfriends or girlfriends, and spouses, as well as betrayal by anyone else we thought we could trust.

It is a hard task to let go of the offense of what someone has done to us. It seems we are letting them off the hook when we feel there should be punishment for what they did to us.

Romans 12:19 (NLT) warns us, *"Dear friends, never take revenge. Leave that to the righteous anger of God. For the Scriptures say, "I will take revenge; I will pay them back," says the Lord.*

Psalm 57:6 (NIV) describes how *"They spread a net for my feet-I was bowed down in distress."*

Whenever we do not forgive, we step into a trap the enemy set for us. With our feet ensnared, we are stuck in the trap of judgment and unforgiveness. We cannot keep walking toward the things God has planned for us. If we are trapped in the same net time after time, we will never enjoy true happiness. Our hopes, dreams, and joy can die in us. What God wants for us is to be free so we can have hope, trust and joy.

In the spiritual realm, unforgiveness is a satanic cord that attaches us to the offending party. It is an open door for the enemy and it allows other spirits like hatred and bitterness to enter as well.

In my own life, I discovered I had a lot of forgiving to do a lot by people whom I should have been able to trust had hurt me. As I learned about forgiveness and studied the Word, I realized I had been playing into the devil's hand and that he was very happy with my entrapment. The Word says, *"My people die from lack of knowledge."* In John 15:21 (NIV), Jesus teaches us, *"They will treat you this way because of my name, for they don't know the one who sent me."* One thing that has helped me a lot on my road to forgiveness is realizing that the spirit in them that hurt me was not the Spirit of God but of the enemy. I can hate the spirit of the enemy in them and not hate the person that God created. If they knew who Jesus was they would not have treated me the way they did. It sends my hurt, anger, and unforgiveness to the right place. I do a lot of counseling with abused women. Statistics show that a high percentage of the perpetrators of abuse were also victims. I am not excusing the behavior of the offenders, but it helps to understand that they did not know about God's forgiveness or His healing touch and that someone who did not know God also hurt them.

John Mason, a best selling author said "unforgiveness does a great deal more damage to the vessel in which it is being stored, than the object to which it is being poured out on." He also stated "People need love most when they deserve it the least."

When Jesus died on the cross, he forgave all of our past, present, and future sins. He loves us when we deserve it the least. Whenever I struggle with unforgiveness, I remember this unidentified author's quote; "Unforgiveness is like drinking poison and waiting for the other person to die." Drink the cup of forgiveness today and be cleansed of the poison of unforgiveness.

Thought for the Day:

Jehovah-Nissi (The Lord my Banner) Please reveal to me everyone I need to forgive. I choose to forgive, I lay it down at the foot of Your cross. Let the banner over me be Forgiveness!

NO TIME

Matthew 11:28-30 (NIV)

Come to me, all who are weary and burdened, and I will give you rest. Take my yoke upon you and learn from me for I am gentle and humble in heart, and you will find rest for your souls, for my yoke is easy and my burden is light.

There are times in our lives when everything seems to be going along smoothly and we feel right with the world. Then, along comes a pin that bursts our bubble and a new reality sets in. We put on our fighting gear, grit our teeth, and prepare for battle.

There is so much pressure on the family today, with both parents working, children suffering the wounds of their parents' divorce, and single moms and dads trying to fulfill the role of both father and mother.

In the midst of it all, where does God fit in when we are already so overwhelmed with all our responsibilities and commitments? We end up physically and emotionally spent by the end of the day. Even though the rest and peace is so close, we are so busy we can't find it.

Most of us know the scriptural basis of tithing. We give our "first fruits" to the Lord. We tend to think of it as a portion of our income, but what we need to remember is that He also wants the "first fruits" of our time as well. It may mean we need to get up earlier in the morning.

The words of Psalm 5:3 (NLT) encourage us; *"Listen to my voice in the morning, LORD. Each morning I bring my requests to you and wait expectantly."*

Once we get in the habit of giving our first fruits of time to God, we will discover our whole day goes better. As we give God the first of our time and draw away from worldly things, we feed our spiritual being. An old hymn says "The things of earth become strangely dim." We can train our minds to have peace through anything the world decides to throw at us if we learn to bask in His presence first.

As I spent time with the Lord today, I began rocking. At first, I didn't even know that I was. When I realized what I was doing, I felt the Lord say that He had rocked me many times in my life and wanted to take me back there for a few moments. He brought to my mind some hard things I had been through, then, through spiritual eyes, I saw Him holding me and rocking me. I felt His presence. He told me to put my hand on my heart and listen. He said that my heart beats with His. He made me in His image. As I felt my heart beating and listened to the sound, I imagined myself in the rocking chair on my Father's lap, my head against His chest, listening to His heartbeat. He was as close to me as my own heart beat. It was a very special time for me and I would have missed it if I had been too busy that day.

I have a plan to buy a rocking chair. It will be a very comfortable chair. I plan to spend a lot of time rocking with my hand on my heart. I don't want to miss this precious time as I listen to my Abba Father's heartbeat in tune with mine.

Thought for the Day:

Jehovah-Shammah (The Lord is there) Forgive me Lord for being so busy with life I forget about the One who is Life. I want to feel You rocking me as a father rocks his favorite child.

RETURN TO ME

Isaiah 44:22 (NLT)

I have swept away your sins like the morning mists. I have scattered your offenses like the clouds. Oh, return to me, for I have paid the price to set you free.

I am a visual person. In this scripture, Isaiah gives me an awesome picture of what forgiveness looks like. I like to just sit and watch the clouds move; they move so quickly. That's how God forgives us, quickly! He doesn't want us to sit in our sin. The wind of His spirit blows away our sins just as the wind blows the clouds quickly past us.

Isaiah also uses the morning mist as a visual concerning our sins. Mist is temporary. Once the light and warmth from the sun touches it, it disappears. If you sleep in, you forfeit the chance of witnessing the sun's effect on the mist, and awake never knowing it occurred. Some of us are still sleeping in and missing what Our Father in Heaven gives us every morning, new mercies. We must wake up and watch the mist disappear as the light of the "Son" melts our sins away.

The Lord says, "Return to me then I will set you free." Meditating on this, I saw a picture of a blackboard. On it were listed all of my sins. Every one you could think of was there. It was disheartening seeing the multitude of them, yet there they were, written out and staring at me. Next, I saw Jesus standing beside me holding an eraser. As He tried to erase the sins, I jumped in front of Him; I didn't want Him to see my sins because I was too ashamed. There was someone else there. It was the enemy offering me a fresh supply of chalk. He wants to continually remind me of my sins so I'll write them down again. Jesus wants me to forget them. Jesus said in Matthew 26:28 (KJV) "For this is my blood of the new testament, which is shed for many for the remission (forgiveness) of sins."

When I was in grade school, one of our jobs was to go outside and clean the erasers. We would clap them together and there would be a cloud of chalk dust all around us. Then the breeze would come and clear the air.

Jesus is holding the eraser. The blood He shed on the cross of Calvary makes it possible for us to stand away from the chalkboard and let Him erase our sins and blow them away like clouds. He has already taken our shame and our guilt, but we must return to Him so that He can set us free. With repentance, Jesus wipes the slate clean.

John 8:36 (NIV) declares to us, *"So If the Son sets you free, you will be free indeed."* It is our choice whether to accept or reject what Jesus did on the cross. Which will you choose the chalk or the eraser?

Thought for the Day:

Jehovah-Tsidkenu (The Lord Our Righteousness) Thank you for wiping my sins away. For me to hold onto them is to say that what I did is greater than what You did. I declare Your righteousness over me.

SACRED SEAL

2 Corinthians 1:22 (NIV)

God set His seal of ownership on us and put His Spirit in our hearts as a deposit guaranteeing what is to come.

Ephesians 1:13 (NIV)

And you also were included in Christ when you heard the word of truth, the gospel of your salvation. Having believed, you were marked in him with a seal, the promised Holy Spirit.

When I was a child, my mom would go grocery shopping and depending on how much money she spent, she would receive green stamps. I remember having to lick those stamps, which tasted awful, and putting them in a stamp book. After you accumulated a certain number of completed stamp books you could look through a gift book and choose a gift. The more stamps you had, the better the gift you could get. The gift book was full of things for the house like tables, lamps, and towels. You knew that if you had the required amount of stamp filled books, you could get the gift pictured in the book.

It is like that with the Holy Spirit. When we accept Him into our lives He moves into our hearts and puts His seal, His stamp of ownership on us. The gift of His Spirit is a promise of more to come. It is His guarantee that He has deposited something in us, that He has changed something in us. We did not have to save stamps or or accomplish any other work. It is a free gift, given from the heart of Jesus.

A stamp or seal to denotes ownership and identity. It represents approval, something of value. How wonderful it is to know that we have been stamped with an irrevocable seal on our heart that says we are the property of the Lord Jesus Christ; which makes us eligible for all the gifts in the Book. When the enemy tries to plead his case against us, we can say we have been sealed and forgiven by the Blood of the Lamb!

The roar of a lion can be heard for a distance of five miles. As the lion roars, he is proclaiming that the land is his and is warning his enemies to stay away. He has claimed his territory; and so has our Lion of Judah, proclaiming us as His territory. His roar pierces the atmosphere declaring His rightful Kingship. It is a warning sound, an audible seal that says, "you are trespassing on my territory, and you must get off. This land has been bought with a price and it is legally mine."

When Jesus died on the cross and went back to be with his Father, He knew that His disciples would miss their dearest friend, leader and master, and that they wouldn't make it on their own without Him. He told his followers to go to the Upper Room and wait upon the Holy Spirit. At Pentecost, they received His Holy Spirit seal and a promise of more to come, for both themselves and future generations of believers. For now, that is enough to claim us as His until we meet face to face and experience His fullness.

Thought for the Day:

Jehovah-Rohi (The Lord is my Shepherd) I praise you. I have been bought with a price and sealed with the kiss of eternity! Thank You Lion of Judah for making me Your very own!

SINGING OVER ME

Zephaniah 3:17 (NIV)

The Lord your God is with you, he is mighty to save. He will take great delight in you, he will quiet you with his love, he will rejoice over you with singing"

I love this scripture because it is so personal. The same God who made the heavens and the earth takes time to sing over us. I remember singing to my children when they were small. Sometimes they would be fussing and crying and I would start to sing and they would calm down. At the time, I didn't realize that as I carried them for nine months they came to know my voice. When I sang to them, the sound of my voice was soothing because it was familiar. It was a sound of comfort and safety.

God wants us to be that familiar with the sound of his voice. He wants us to know it so well that we can recognize it and run to him when we need to be comforted and feel safe.

When we take the time to know His voice, we will be able to hear the song He is longing to sing to us. We must take the time and listen to hear "our song." Why would He sing over us if we cannot hear him? His song is unlike any song we have ever heard. It is an intimate song, created even before we were born and it is just for us. No one will have the same song as you. You are special in your Father's eyes and you will have a special song.

My son and his new bride had their customary first dance together. They spent a long time picking out "their" song, a song that meant something special to them and their relationship. It is such a beautiful time at a wedding to watch the bride and groom dance that first dance together as man and wife. Watching them reminded me of how our Heavenly Father desires to have that first dance with us, singing the song He chose for His Bride. Close your eyes and listen as the One who loves you, rejoices over "His bride" with singing!

Thought for the Day:

El Shaddai (Lord God Almighty) What an amazing God You are! I long to hear You sing over me. Prepare me for my wedding day where we can dance and sing for eternity.

SPRING CLEANING

John 15:1-2 (NLT)

"I am the true vine, and my Father is the gardener. He cuts off every branch that doesn't produce fruit, and he prunes the branches that do bear fruit so they will produce even more."

As I thought about starting my dreaded spring-cleaning, I began to reminisce of childhood days when my mom would do her spring-cleaning. I can honestly say I have never cleaned my house like my mom did. She would take one room at a time, sometimes only getting through one room in a day. I remember that my mother would decide which job my sister, my brothers, and I would do, depending upon our size at the time. Since I was the youngest, I got to clean the baseboards. My taller siblings would help with washing the walls. The curtains came down, windows were washed, and our dresser drawers gone through to sort out all the clothes we had outgrown. My mom would wrap an old rag around a brush with a long handle to get down all the hard to reach cobwebs. Every nook and cranny was cleaned. It was a time we children wanted no part of, yet I still remember how clean and fresh everything smelled when we were finished.

One day, as I was journaling to the Lord, I saw a picture of a box and a key. At first, I wasn't sure what He was trying to show me, but I kept listening. I heard in my spirit that when we ask Jesus to come into our hearts, He moves in and what He finds in many of us is a locked box. That box holds the past; the memories we would like to forget, the failures, anything we don't want anyone else to see.

We lock that box, hold onto the key, then hide the box making sure no one can access it. We think that if we hide it away, like we do with unwanted things in a spare bedroom, *we* will even forget it is there. Sometimes it works, but other times, when we least expect it, a situation or conversation will occur that reminds of us what is in our box. No longer hidden, it is right out in front of us where we must face it once more.

We are all willing to let Jesus come into our heart and do the maintenance cleaning, a little dusting here, some reorganizing over there. But when it comes to the deep down cleaning; taking down the blinds and the curtains, scrubbing the walls, and sorting through all our old stuff, we keep the spare bedroom locked up with all of our junk and our box hidden, never to be looked at or used.

When we ask Jesus into our hearts (born again), He wants us to give Him not only our heart but also the key to the box. His desire is to do a spiritual housecleaning. Not just dusting around the edges but the kind of cleaning my mom did. I have a feeling my mother probably gave Him a few pointers! He wants to take down the blinds and the curtains and wash the windows of our souls. The old clothes of the world that don't fit us anymore are exchanged for robes of righteousness. He takes the Sword of the Spirit and cuts down the cobwebs that are blocking His light from shining through us.

As we give Him the key and allow Him to clean our "house", He will blow His spirit through the rooms. It will smell clean and fresh. Then we can open up the spare bedroom that was once off limits and fill it with company, the company of the Father, Son, and Holy Spirit.

Thought for the Day:

Jehovah-Rapha, (The Lord Who Heals) I welcome You into my "House." Do a work in every area of my being. I give You the key to every room, even the rooms that say "Do Not Enter!" I want You to do a total cleaning so that I can be set free.

THE ANT

Matthew 17:20 (NIV)

He replied, "Because you have so little faith. I tell you the truth, if you have faith as small as a mustard seed, you can say to this mountain, 'Move from here to there' and it will move. Nothing will be impossible for you."

It was a beautiful autumn day as I sat on my swing in the backyard. I love to sit out there when I need to get away from life and put everything back into perspective.

While I was sitting there, something moving on the ground got my attention. It was a large wood chip moving at a high rate of speed. Upon closer inspection I saw that a tiny ant was dragging it. I watched the ant negotiate a thick cable in its path. As it approached what must have looked like a mountain, there was no hesitation; in a second the ant scaled the cable, wood chip still in tow. Within minutes, it had gone a great distance. I watched intently as the little ant plowed through every obstacle, determined to get his cargo to its destination.

My spirit began to stir as I felt the Lord speaking to me about what I just saw. When an obstacle got in the ant's way, there was no stopping and weighing the possibility of failure or success, only sheer determination to get the job done. God is calling us to think differently. We all have our own obstacles. Perhaps it's a broken marriage, or a mountain of debt that seems impossible to climb.

In Deuteronomy 20:4 (NLT), it says, "*For the Lord your God is going with you. He will fight against your enemies, and give you victory.*"

59

In Deuteronomy 1:20 (NLT), Moses says, *"You have now reached the land that the Lord our God is giving us. Look! He has placed it in front of you. Don't be afraid! Don't be discouraged! But you responded; first, let's send out scouts to explore the land for us."*

As the Israelites got close to the Promised Land, fear overcame them. They had traveled with Moses since leaving Egypt. They had a cloud by day and a pillar of fire by night to lead them. Manna fell from heaven to feed them. Their clothing and shoes never wore out yet they still could not jump over the cable into their promised land. Twelve scouts were sent out to check out the situation. They returned with delicious fruit claiming it was indeed a good land. But...(There are always the **buts** in our life that hold us back) they cried, *"Why shall we go there? We are afraid. The men we sent tell us that the people are stronger and taller than we are. They saw giants there."* Only two of the twelve, Joshua and Caleb, had the faith to go back there.

God had so much He wanted to give His chosen people. Their murmurings, fears, disbelief, and disobedience prevented them from ever experiencing what a good Father had planned to give His children. The Israelites who fled Egypt wandered the desert for forty years and died never having seen or enjoyed the land of milk and honey they had spent their lives searching for; and it was right in front of them. Only Joshua, Caleb and the next generation entered in.

What giants are keeping you from your Promised Land, insecurities, fear of failure, listening to the advice of man? We must be as focused as the ant and as faithful as Joshua and Caleb. We cannot look at the size of the obstacle, or be frightened away by the would-be giants. We must do as David did with Goliath. It only took one smooth stone to knock the life out of Goliath. Reach in your pocket, pull out a stone of faith, and trust the power behind it.

Thought for the Day:

Jehovah-Nissi (The Lord is my Banner) Today I place my fears, discouragements, fear of failure, at the foot of Your cross. I declare in the Name above all names, that nothing will stop me from reaching my Promised Land!

THE DANCE OF LIFE

Psalm 30:11 (NLT)

You have turned my mourning into joyful dancing.

I remember the night I went to my first prom I received a little keepsake, a book to write the names of those with whom I danced. It was a reminder of that special night.

That was many years ago, a faint memory. Yesterday, as I sat quietly and listened for the "still, small voice", I heard "Come and join me in a dance of a lover and His bride. Let me dance you through the trials of this world." He was going to fill up every line in my book as we danced the dance of life. I was to get so used to His arms encircling me that I would run to them whenever I needed to feel safe. It was a vision I will never forget.

When I dance with my husband, I have a tendency to start leading. In my vision with the Lord, I was reminded that I was not to lead I was to follow. I saw myself dancing with Jesus, and underneath our feet were all my worldly problems, concerns, and fears. They seemed unimportant as He swept me over them. He told me to look deep into His eyes as lovers do when they dance. For me to look away and lose my gaze would mean I would be looking at the world and not at Him.

David, who eventually became the King of Israel, wrote most of the Psalms. He had many trying situations in his life and yet his Psalms are full of praise from a worshipper's heart, and intimacy with his Father. As we saw in Psalm 30:11 above he wrote, "You have turned my mourning into joyful dancing."

The Bible tells us that David danced through the streets as he entered the City of David. In 2 Samuel 6:14 (NLT) it says, "And David danced before the Lord with all his might."

Paul and Silas were thrown into a filthy, dark prison cell after being severely flogged. It is written that they were singing praises and the other prisoners were listening. I can imagine them dreamily dancing in the spirit, envisioning a time when they would be able to dance before the Lord free from the shackles that bound them. We are told in Acts 16:26 that suddenly, a violent earthquake shook the foundation of the prison; the doors of the prison flew open and the chains of every prisoner fell off!

When the world beats us up and we are bound by worries, hurt, shame, and fear, could it be that if we praised and danced to our Creator, our prison doors would fly open and our chains would fall off?

Now as I study my Bible, and I read about the stoning of Stephen, and of John, a prisoner on the Isle of Patmos, I get a better understanding of how they endured such persecution yet continued to praise God through it all. They had been so used to being in His presence, praising, dancing, and singing, that no matter what circumstances came their way, they went to that familiar place of safety where they were swept off their feet as they gazed into the eyes of the lover of their souls.

Jesus is reaching out His hand to us, inviting us to dance the dance of life. He never intended us to be on our own, He created us to have a relationship with Him. He is longing to sweep us off our feet, drawing us ever deeper in love with Him.

He is asking you right now, "May I have the next dance?"

Thought for the Day:

Jehovah-Shalom (The Lord Is Peace) Thank you Lord for loving me so much. I grow weary of the challenges of this journey on earth. Sweep me away to that peaceful, intimate place above the cares of this world.

THE GOOD SHEPHERD

John 10:14-16 (NLT)

*"I am the good shepherd; I know my own sheep, and they know
me, just as my Father knows me and I know the Father. And I lay
down my life for the sheep. I have other sheep, too, that are not in
this sheepfold. I must bring them also, and they will listen to my
voice; and there will be one flock and one shepherd.*

Here are some facts about sheep: They wander, they
get lost, and they get stuck in thickets. If a sheep
tries to go through a hole in the fence and the hole
is too small, he will keep trying to go forward instead of backing
out. If a sheep jumps off a cliff, the others are likely to follow. That
is why sheep cannot survive without a shepherd.

Its no wonder Jesus compared us to sheep! We can get
lost and off the path without too much trouble and become caught
in the thickets of life. Just like the sheep, we tend keep doing the
same thing expecting a different result. How many times have we
done things that we know are wrong but choose to follow the
crowd and jump into disaster?

Some of us start out on the right path and then someone or
something pulls us off track. The moment we deviate from the
original path and turn our foot in the other direction, we get lost.
The longer we stay lost, the more we seem to get into trouble.
There aren't many rules in this new direction and it is very enticing
at first. We begin to make new friends and to leave the old ones
behind. New habits replace old as we stray further and further

away, slowly heading straight for destruction. For most people there comes a time when they wake up and realize their mistake. They find it's not so easy to get back to the flock they left behind. Time and distance have taken their toll.

Revelation 12:10 warns us about the accuser of the brethren. Once he has the evidence he needs, he begins to build a case against us, a case built with guilt and shame. When we realize that we have been on the wrong path and decide to change direction, the old friendly wolf in sheep's clothing is suddenly not so friendly. He is not going to let us out of the trap without a fight. Even though we have decided to change our ways, the not so friendly wolf meets us at the crossroads again and says, "You can't change now, think of everything you've done." He has already robbed us of relationship, destroyed marriages, families, and most importantly, the relationship with the Shepherd who wants to bring us back into the fold where He can watch over us. We come to Him broken and bruised, weak and weary. Just as He carried the weight of our sin on the cross, he picks us up the lost sheep and carries it on his shoulders. He doesn't want to risk losing us again. He washes us, feeds us the Word and loves us. To Him, it is as though we never left.

Jesus longs to guide us down the path that is right for our lives as only the Good Shepherd can. He loves us so much that if we get lost He will leave the other ninety-nine to go find us. Even as He watches over His sheep, he is constantly looking out for that one lost sheep.

Rev. 7:17 For the Lamb at the center of the throne will be their shepherd; 'he will lead them to springs of living water.' 'And God will wipe away every tear from their eyes.'"

At last, we are home in the safety of our Shepherd's arms!

Thought for the Day:

Jehovah-Raah (The Lord My Shepherd) Lord, just like those sheep, I have wandered away, following my own path, trying to figure out everything myself. It was there that I realized how much I needed a Savior. I choose to follow You, my Shepherd.

THE GREAT RESCUER

Psalm 18:16-19 (NLT)

He reached down from heaven and rescued me;
He drew me out of deep waters.
He delivered me from my powerful enemies, from those who
hated me and were too
strong for me.
They attacked me at a moment when I was weakest,
But the Lord upheld me, He led me to a place of safety; he
rescued me because he
delights in me.

While sitting at the beach, I watched as the waves formed frothy white caps, piling on top of one another and coming to a crashing crescendo. As each wave broke apart, it gracefully made its way to the shoreline. The tide transported seaweed and ocean debris, depositing it onto the sand, and then returned it to the sea. This cycle repeated itself over and over again. Oftentimes I think we also repeat cycles in our life over and over again. We keep making the same mistakes, and when we try to fight the current on our own, we eventually weaken and are pulled further out into the deep.

When I watch surfers, I love how they glide over the top of the waves and the powerful force below them. It seems effortless and picturesque but when the unexpected force of nature knocks them off balance, they go crashing down. In a moment the picture changes from having mastered the forces of nature to chaos, as arms, legs and surfboard all go in different directions. It is a great parallel to our "ride" here on planet earth. Just when we think we have life figured out, something or someone comes along and knocks us off our board, and off we go into a sea of chaos. Learning is a process and once in a while we get thrown off our board and reminded of our weakness.

I have almost drowned twice. Just as I needed someone to rescue me in those times, there have been many times since when I felt as though I was drowning in the overpowering current of life and needed someone to come and save me. Through those times I have come to know the Great Rescuer. He has pulled me out of the currents that tried to pull me under and has resuscitated me, blowing the breath of the Holy Spirit back into me.

Psalm 42:7 (NLV) *I hear the tumult of the raging seas as your waves and surging tides sweep over me.*
Psalm 56:13 (NLV) *For you have rescued me from death; You have kept my feet from slipping. So now I can walk in your presence, O God, In your life giving light.*
Psalm 57:1 (NLV) *Have mercy on me, O God, have mercy! I look to you for protection. I will hide beneath the shadow of your wings until this violent storm is past.*

Having had my share of "near drowning experiences", I have learned that there are times in my life when I cannot rescue myself, though I tried with everything I had to reach the shore. The more I tried the weaker my arms got and the force of the water pulled me further out. By God's grace I didn't drown. Many of us have been taught to handle our problems and to be self-reliant. Asking for help would show weakness. That is opposite to what our Rescuer says we should do. He wants for us to come to Him as children. Children need someone to protect them.

Now I know to ask for help and when I am rescued I am ready to take the time to lie on the beach and rest in the warmth of the "Son's" love. I will wait until He takes my hand and says it is safe to go back in the water.

Thought for the Day:

Jehovah-Shammah (The Lord Is There) Thank you Lord that You have never failed to catch me when I'm about to fall, you are my comforter, the ONE who takes great delight in being my rescuer!

THE PAGES OF OUR LIVES

Exodus 17:14 (NLT)

Then the Lord instructed Moses, "Write this down as a permanent record, and announce it to Joshua:

Malachi 3:16 (NLT Holy Spirit Encounter)

Then those who feared LORD spoke with each other, and the LORD listened to what they said. In his presence, a scroll of remembrance was written to record the names of those who feared him and loved to think about him.

Being a writer, I was so excited to discover these two scriptures. I never noticed them before, but I have thought about them a lot since uncovering them. I believe that God is excited about books. After all, not only did He give us the books of the Old and New Testament, He has "permanent records"; the Lamb's Book of Life, and a book of remembrance for each believer.

Above, in Malachi 3:16 we get a glimpse of the Lord listening in on a conversation shared by those who love Him. When He heard His name mentioned, it was so important to Him that He made sure to have these precious words recorded.

When we are born again, our names are written in the "Lamb's Book of Life". I am telling you, He is really into this book thing. Picture judgment day; you come before the King, and He checks to see if your name is in His book. If it isn't written there, it is down the hatch you go. That book is the most important book of our lives. It is a book of life or death.

I believe He is writing a personal non-fiction book about each of our lives to look through with us when we meet Him face to face. Some of our books may be more like suspense novels; others like mysteries or love stories, but not all will have a happy ending.

One day I was feeling bad about not being appreciated, aching for some words of encouragement. I decided to write in my journal and inquire of my Abba father about my feelings. He told me that man's opinions and praises were fleeting and worthless, and that the need for man's approval was not His design but was planted by the enemy. He said that the enemy knows how short lived and fickle that type of adulation is but also knows what an addictive attraction it has.

Then He revealed a few memories that were already in my book. There is the time that one of the homeless women told me she liked my new earrings. She had so little that I not only gave her the earrings but the dress that matched. They were brand new and were my favorite, it was hard to part with them. He noticed. He said that each time I counseled, prayed with, and listened to one of His children, even though I was exhausted and felt like I had nothing more to give, He noticed. He reminded me of the ups and downs I had experienced being a wife, a mother, and a friend. I was faithful to my calling, He noticed. He recalled the hard times I had had throughout my life and how I would always pick myself up again and never give up, He noticed. Just as we like to keep baby books, pictures and growth charts of our children, watching them grow and mature, our heavenly Father does the same with us throughout our lives.

I realized that God sees the sacrifices we make in order to reflect His image. I no longer feel the need for any man to give me his approval. I only have the desire to create a lot of good memories that my Father in heaven will notice, and instruct the angels to record in "My Book"!

Thought for the Day:

Adonai (Lord, Master) Lord, let today be a day that I make memories for "My Book"! Open my eyes to see what You see, my ears to hear what You hear, and my heart to feel what You feel over Your children today.

THE SEIGE IS OVER

2 Samuel 22:18 (NLT)

He rescued me from my powerful enemies, from those who hated me and were too strong for me.

Psalm 31:21(NLT)

Praise the LORD, for he has shown me the wonders of his unfailing love. He kept me safe when my city was under attack.

For some time, I had been battling a health issue. It hit me very hard. Just when I felt I was getting better, It would hit me again. It dragged on for what seemed like forever. I have always lived a very active life. Now I had to stop and do nothing. It was a struggle and I had to seek the Lord for strength and patience.

One morning I woke up hearing the phrase, "The siege is over." I heard it repeatedly as I went about my day. I did not hear the battle is over or the war is over, but that the siege is over. As I pondered it, I realized the Lord was teaching me something. What I had been going through for all that time was a siege. The enemy didn't attack me by a frontal assault, he knows I am wise to his schemes. He also knows that I would refuse to surrender.

A siege is typically an act by the enemy to surround the target. It can also mean a long season of illness. Sieges involve below the belt, deceptive methods like blocking routes so that food and water can't get in. In days past, the enemy, knowing that those they were sieging were getting weak and vulnerable to disease, would catapult diseased animals over city walls to further weaken their opponents.

The word siege comes from the Latin word for seat or sitting. The enemy will "sit" and wait until he weakens you enough to conquer you. He waits patiently for the white flag of surrender. Time is on his side, as he knows that with each passing day you will become an easier target, as you get weaker and weaker.

This siege was a very strong test for me. I came close to checking out all together. The attack came in such a way that whatever I ate would not stay down or in. Even water wouldn't stay down and I became dangerously dehydrated. I was actually starving and overcome by disease. I felt as though I were surrounded on every side. My spirit was weakened. The siege had all but defeated me.

The holding of a strong defensive position by one party characterizes siege warfare. I was the one who was holding a strong position. Reaching within I found no strength. I tried to pick up my sword to do battle but I didn't have the strength, it was just out of my reach. I then heard the Lord say, "Even at your weakest point you are still more powerful than your enemy, pick up your sword." I had a notepad next to me, My enemy didn't fool me for long. I simply wrote Jesus help me, Jesus help me. He answered my prayer and taught me how to overcome a siege. I used the sword of the Spirit and quoted scriptures like, "I can do all things through Christ who strengthens me." I didn't raise the white flag and surrender.

Many Godly people prayed for me, including a praying husband and family. God hears the cries of faithful prayers. We need to be surrounded by people of faith so they can rally around us with their swords when we're too weak to fight alone.

I am now stronger and wise to another tactic of the enemy. I have the Word planted deep in my soul so that when I don't have the strength to pick up a Bible, the Word is still available because it is written in my heart.

When we are under siege, surrender is not an option. We must press on until we hear the words "The siege is over."

Thought for the Day:

Jehovah-Sabaoth (The Lord Of Hosts) Lion of the Tribe of Judah, help us to be victorious over every plan, scheme and siege that the enemy directs at me. Strengthen every weak place; fortify every wall, for You are the author and finisher of our faith.

THE SHADOW OF YOUR WINGS

Psalm 57:1 (NIV)

Have mercy on me, O God, have mercy on me, for in you my soul takes refuge. I will take refuge in the shadow of your wings until the disaster has passed.

D isaster is a good word for what I had been going through for that couple of weeks. It started when I went to the dentist and he discovered I had an abscess tooth and it would need to be pulled. The procedure went smoothly and everything seemed to be normal. I was not expecting the events that followed.

The dentist gave me a prescription for antibiotics. I started taking them and almost immediately began to feel sick. I had a sudden, severe reaction to them and I ended up in the hospital.

It was a very hard time for my husband and me. We had no insurance and he missed a lot of work taking care of me. Once I returned home from the hospital, I felt better, but within a few days, the symptoms that had put me in the hospital came rushing back. A spirit of fear engulfed me.

As I lay on that bed, filled with fear, I cried out to the Lord. He brought to my memory the scripture 1 Peter 5:8 (NLT), "Your enemy, The Devil, roams around like a roaring lion, looking for someone to devour." I thought, "I must look like easy prey for a hungry lion."

I declared war immediately. I got up, put on my warfare music, and began to dance and proclaim the healing that Jesus had won for us on the cross. My arms and legs were very shaky at first, but as I continued to dance, the weakness began to leave. I would rest intermittently, and I gradually began to feel the Lord's presence overtaking me. I literally felt like He was pulling a hungry lion off me. As I continued to dance all of the symptoms left me, I heard in my spirit that I was His warrior and that through this experience I would come to know that I could do all things through Christ who strengthens me.

Throughout this terrible battle He had sheltered me in the shadow of His wings, and had kept me there until the disaster had passed. Sometimes I would fight, and sometimes I would rest and the battle was His.

I realized that even as God had given me the strength to be a victorious warrior. I could also rest in His arms as He destroyed the enemy on my behalf.

Deuteronomy 33:27 (NKJ)

The eternal God is your refuge, and underneath are the everlasting arms; He will thrust out the enemy from before you, and will say, 'Destroy!'

Thought for the Day:
Yahweh (I Am) I thank you that You are Yahweh-my place of refuge and protection. You are my shield and buckler, my defense. Thank You that I dwell in the secret place in the shelter of the Most High.

THE TURTLE SHELL

Psalm 18:2 (NIV)

The Lord is my rock, my fortress and my deliverer; my God is my rock, in whom I take refuge, my shield and the horn of my salvation, my stronghold.

While playing a game of cards with my husband, I suddenly felt the presence of the Lord over me. I saw His hand, bidding me to come. I told my husband and went to be alone with the Lord. I said "Lord, where do you want me to go? I will go anywhere you want me to." I heard in my spirit, "I want you to come out of where you are." At first, I didn't understand, then I saw a picture from years ago in my spirit.

When I was about fifteen, I was in Shriner's Hospital because of severe scoliosis. They put a body cast from the top of my head to the top of my legs that I wore for three months. I will never forget the day they took it off; they used a power saw! It was very loud and scary. When the cast was removed, I got off the table; it was hard to keep my balance. I felt like I was going to float away. I didn't notice the weight of the cast until they removed it.

The Lord showed me that memory like a parable. He said that that we sometimes put casts or shells on ourselves. The process can begin in early childhood, especially if we feel unprotected. Made up of hurts, pain, rejection, abuse, and fears that have been slowly loaded onto us, our shell goes unnoticed. Wearing it becomes both ritual and habit. Our shell of protection not only blocks our emotions and pain, but also the ability to love or feel God in the fullest sense.

I thought about a turtle and how our Creator encased it with a shell. It is hard and strong, almost impenetrable. Anytime the turtle senses danger, he can hide in that shell for safety. You can pick him up and try to make him come out but he won't budge until he feels completely safe.

Though our Creator did not make us with a shell, many of us fashion our own, as rock hard as the turtle's. We hide in it never leaving its safety. Feeling it is better to stay right there rather than taking the risk of trusting and being hurt, our hearts become hard and impenetrable just like the shell.

How do you suppose the turtle would feel if we were to take it out of its shell? The words that come to my mind are vulnerable, scared, exposed. Isn't that exactly how we would feel if we were to remove our shells? It's been safe in there for a long time. Isn't it better to just stay in there? That way nobody gets hurt. Who knows what would happen if I were to come out? Yes, it's best to just leave things the way they are.

That is what I thought too until the Lord asked me to "Come out of where I was." He wanted me to leave the shell behind, to trust Him. He was all I would need. I would no longer need the shell to protect me. I agreed to leave my own protective shell behind, to become vulnerable. He showed me that outside my shell were gifts He had for me, which I would never have gotten had I not stripped off my shell. Just as I had felt like a feather with my half-body cast removed I now felt a new, light, spiritual freedom. Abba Father had taken all the weight I had been carrying for years.

Matthew 11:30 (NIV) states, "For my yoke is easy and my burden is light." That tells me that God gives us each a choice to come out of our shell and put our trust in Him. He is asking you the same question that He asked me. "Will you come out of where you are?"

Thought for the Day:

Elohim (Creator, Mighty and Strong, My Protection My Provision) Lord I want to fully trust in You. My own walls, shells and veils are only illusions that temporarily trick me into believing that I can protect myself. You alone are my hiding place, my rock and my strong tower.

THE VINE

2 Corinthians 11:14 (NLT)

But I am not surprised! Even Satan can disguise himself as an angel of light.

While weeding my garden one day, I noticed that vines had wrapped themselves around most of my flowers. They had shiny, delicate looking leaves. But, as I tried to separate them from my flowers, I realized they weren't delicate at all, *and* they were strangling my flowers. When I tried to uproot them they would break off at ground level. I would then untangle the vines from my flowers but they always grew back, choking my plants and stopping them from blooming. I got tired of the constant struggle, so one day I followed the vine to its source and dug up the ground. I discovered a large hard bulb. It had attached itself to the roots of one of my plants. Although invisible to the eye, it was slowly draining the life out of my plant. I broke my gardening tool trying to remove it. I decided to leave it exposed to the sun until the next day. To my surprise, the exposure to the light had weakened the bulb and I was able to pull it right out.

As I wrestled with these vines, the Lord showed me a parallel of what the enemy does to us. God created us to blossom and thrive. The seed of His word is planted in us. But if we don't tend our garden, the enemy sows vines of rejection, offense, and ridicule. We, like the plants, are overtaken by vines that entangle us and rob us of life so we can't get back to the Master Gardener. We can look great on the outside, but on the inside we are slowly dying. Just like the vine bound plant, it's just a matter of time before our leaves begin to wither and fall.

That is why we must read God's Word to learn who we really are. It is our weed killer against the wiles of the enemy. Satan tries to wrap himself around our roots, our innermost thoughts, starve us and eventually choke the life right out of us. He uses fear of failure and humiliation to weaken our faith, and make us doubt God's promises with lies like "You're a failure", "You'll never change", and "God could never forgive you for what you've done." We must expose every lie to the "Light".

Unlike flowers, we have the power to cut away those lies. Pick up God's Word, the Sword of the Spirit from Ephesians 6:17 and cut away every choking vine. Light dispels darkness. Ask Jesus to shine His light and on the root of anything that is not His and break the enemy's hold. Ask the Lord to tend to every place lies were allowed to take root. You will bloom like never before, brightly reflecting the beauty and light of Jesus.

By following a few simple gardening steps, we can be like the beautiful garden in Isaiah 58:11 (NIV), "*The Lord will guide you always, he will satisfy your needs in a sun scorched land and will strengthen your frame, you will be like a well-watered garden, like a spring whose waters never fail.*"

Here is how the Master Gardener produces new growth and beautiful flowers:

1. We must be watered by the Holy Spirit.
John 7:38 (NLT) *"If you believe in Me come and drink! For the scriptures declare that rivers of living water will flow out from within."*

2. We must walk in the Light of the Lord.
John 8:12 (NLT) *"Then Jesus spoke to them again saying 'I am the light of the world. If you follow me you won't be stumbling around through the darkness because you will have the light that leads to life.' "*

3. **We must have good soil.**
Matthew 13:23 (NIV) *"But the one who received the seed that fell on good soil is the man who hears the word and understands it."*

Thought for the Day:
Jehovah-Rapha (The Lord That Heals) Lord, let this be the day that I am set free from the enemy's grip. I want to be that beautiful bloom you created me to be, loosed from every entanglement.

THE WEDDING

Revelation 19:7(NLT)

Let us be glad and rejoice and honor him. For the time has come for the wedding feast of the Lamb, and his bride has prepared herself.

As I walked down the aisle to meet my husband to be, all the plans and preparations leading up to this day were forgotten. I wondered if he would think I was the most beautiful bride he had ever seen. He turned with a look of excitement to get the first glimpse of his new bride. When our eyes met, I was immediately filled with love and acceptance. His eyes said you are even more beautiful than I could have imagined.

Now, it is thirty-two years later. I look back on that day with such joy. Yet, I long for another groom to be waiting at the end of the aisle for me. He will also be looking for His beautiful, spotless bride. He will look at me with eyes of acceptance. The mistakes, the times I chose to go my own way all forgotten. He will smile at me with approval as He takes my hand in His.

The longing of my heart is to be with my Father, Creator and Husband. When I ask Him, "Why must I wait so long to be with the One I love?" He patiently explains to me that just as a baby must have nine months to fully develop in the womb, I must trust His perfect timing to come for His bride. As my Bridegroom is preparing our new home, I must ready myself for His coming.

John 14:2 (NIV)

In my Father's house are many rooms; if it were not so, I would have told you. I am going there to prepare a place for you. And if I go and prepare a place for you, I will come back and take you to be with me that you also may be where I am.

He also calls me to help others equip themselves for the day when the Bridegroom will come for them. We are all in a sense groomsmen and bridesmaids. We are to be servants to one another, helping each other to get prepared for our own wedding day.

Revelation 19:9 (NIV)

Then the angel said to me, "Write: Blessed are those who are invited to the wedding supper of the Lamb!" And he added, "These are the true words of God."

When I am finally standing in my white flowing gown before Him, He will lift back the veil of this world. I will look into His eyes and the longing of my heart will be fulfilled. He will carry me across the threshold between heaven and earth. The bride and her Bridegroom, married for eternity.

Thought for the Day:

Jehovah-Mekoddishkem (The Lord Who Sanctifies You) clothe me with the garments of salvation and robes of righteousness; make me a bride who is ready for her Bridegroom.

THE GREAT I AM

Exodus 3:14

God replied to Moses, "I AM WHO I AM." Say this to the people of Israel: I AM has sent me to you."

While journaling one day, I heard the Lord say "You must come to the knowledge of who I am." He said the world is seemingly spinning out of control for those who don't know Me. Evil will abound and seem like it is lurking around every corner. He gave me instructions to write down all the promises in His Word of who He is.

I Am the bread of life.

I Am the Light of the world.

I Am the door of the sheep.

I Am the Son of God.

I Am the resurrection and the life.

I Am the truth and the life.

I Am the true vine, and my Father is the vinedresser.

I Am Alpha and Omega, says the Lord God, "who is and who was and who is to come, the Almighty.

I Am the first and the last.

He said to declare these truths whenever I feel the weight of the world on my shoulders. As I speak them out loud, they will empower me. When I have the truth of who He is, I will not let the things of this earth wear me down but rather I will wear down the enemy.

In Mark 8 (NIV), Jesus was walking with his disciples. He asked them, "Who do people say I am? They replied, "Some say John the Baptist; others say Elijah; and still others, one of the prophets." " But what about you?" he asked. "Who do you say I am?" Peter answered, "You are the Messiah."

At the crucifixion, a Roman centurion at the foot of the cross was quoted as saying "Surely this man was the Son of God." The question He has for all of us is, "Who do you say I Am?"

Thought for the Day:

Immanuel (I Am) I say that You are my everything. You are the living Son of God and my Father, Creator, the One who died so I could live. I long for the day when I will meet You and live with You for eternity.

❧ ABOUT THE AUTHOR ❧

Susan is a licensed pastor, spiritual counselor, and freelance writer. Her life experiences are the foundation of her writing. Susan has served countless hours in spiritual counseling watching God set captives free; including pastors and leaders as well as the lost and homeless. Her vision is to help others through what God has taught her through experience, her teachings and her books. She loves to speak to groups about the unconditional love of the Father, forgiveness and knowing our true identity. She has also written poetry for the pro-life movement and has been published in Maggie Mae Magazine. Susan co-led Transitions Ministry to the Homeless of Central Florida with her husband Steven from 2004 to 2014.

Having completed Short Stories For The Long Road, Susan is now working on publishing a series of three children's books which follow the main character, Milo, as he gains victory over bullying and peer pressure, gains an understanding of adoptive family, and befriends and encourages someone struggling with a physical handicap and abuse. The Milo series will be a great tool for helping children understand and cope with these very real situations in the modern day life of a child.

Susan was born and raised in Massachusetts, and moved to Orlando Florida in 1990. She has been married to her husband, Steven, for thirty-three years, has three children and five grandchildren.

25496817R00059

Made in the USA
Columbia, SC
04 September 2018